THE BECOMING OF GOD

Process Theology, Philosophy, and Multireligious Engagement

ROLAND FABER

 CASCADE *Books* • Eugene, Oregon

THE BECOMING OF GOD
Process Theology, Philosophy, and Multireligious Engagement

Cascade Companions 34

Cascade Books
An Imprint of Wipf and Stock Publishers
199 W. 8th Ave., Suite 3
Eugene, OR 97401

www.wipfandstock.com

PAPERBACK ISBN: 978-1-60608-885-2
HARDCOVER ISBN: 978-1-4982-8588-9
EBOOK ISBN: 978-1-4982-0217-6

Cataloguing-in-Publication data:

Names: Faber, Roland.

Title: The becoming of God : process theology, philosophy, and multireligious engagement / Roland Faber.

Description: Eugene, OR: Cascade Books, 2017 | Series: Cascade Companions.

Identifiers: ISBN 978-1-60608-885-2 (paperback) | ISBN 978-1-4982-8588-9 (hardcover) | ISBN 978-1-4982-0217-6 (ebook)

Subjects: LCSH: process theology | philosophy | multiculturalism—religious aspects

Classification: BT83.6 .F25 2017 (paperback) | BT83.6 .F25 2016 (ebook)

Manufactured in the U.S.A.   03/28/17

THE BECOMING
OF GOD

CONTENTS

CONTOURS TO COME

IN A WAY, THIS book is meant to be an introduction into process theology. This is not an easy endeavor. Process theology is a quite complex phenomenon. It has roots in different philosophical and religious traditions as well as resonances with certain scientific areas and questions. It was pursued for different reasons—be they existential or intellectual, cosmological or spiritual, or any combination of them. It exhibits a varied and variegated history and presents itself as irreducible to one simple motive or outcome. Furthermore, on deeper reflection, process theology cannot be grasped without awareness of its profound connections with a vast field of human, and maybe cosmic, experiences formed in a long process of evolution into, and of, different, long-standing cultural settings. Nevertheless, when we speak of process theology—despite everything we could add to say about it—we cannot do so without mentioning one name and one man's work: that of the Anglo-American mathematician and philosopher Alfred North Whitehead (1861–1947).

Born into an Anglican family residing in Ramsgate, England, with a history of holding religious and missionary offices, he entertained a personal leaning towards Catholicism, especially because of his fondness for Cardinal Newman. Eventually, he lost his faith in the classical image of an omnipotent creator God, as he could not reconcile it with the pain of the death of his son North in the First World War. Professionally, he mastered physical (applied) mathematics in Cambridge, where he became a fellow and lecturer. After the colossal failure of the project reducing mathematics to logics, and creating symbolic logic *eu passant*, manifest in the cooperation with Bertrand Russell on the unparalleled *Principia Mathematica*, he ventured more deeply into philosophy of science. Engaging the new physics of his day, namely, relativity theory and quantum physics, he concentrated his efforts to the overcoming of the scientific materialism of the nineteenth century, which was (and maybe is) still vastly underpinning the scientific outlook, but was called into question with the revolutions of the new physics itself. In the course of this work, Whitehead ended up creating a new organic and processual paradigm for the integration of science and religion, evolution and civilization through the sensitive service of (a new) philosophy—his "philosophy of organism." Developing this new metaphysics or "speculative philosophy" of organism, process, and relationality, he was, after having retired, called to fill a professorship in philosophy at Harvard. He attracted philosophers, scientists, and theologians interested in the application of his innovative views on the intersection between religion and divinity, cosmology and society, initiating the complex and diversified tradition called process theology.

Given this history of origination, a further comment is meaningful at this point. Taking into account the current philosophical and theological sensitivities for the postmodern and postcolonial, gender, and liberation discourses, this birth story of process theology might appear, to some at least, to be of a great disadvantage (or, if you are on the side of the defenders of modernity and its integrity, perhaps, more of a seeming advantage?) since the combination of the historical, social, racial, and intellectual location of Whitehead must leave at least the dim impression of a grave limitation. Wasn't Whitehead a white, male scientist and philosopher, who was educated in and eventually taught at the elite universities of England and America, namely, Cambridge and Harvard? Wouldn't that seem to exemplify almost a striking case of archetypical Eurocentric limitations imposed a priori on anything he and his work would have to say? And would not this impression even be heightened by the fact that his interest was in metaphysics, a highly abstract enterprise, steeped in general notions and claims about everything (or anything at all), which many culturally sensitive persons nowadays deem outdated, that is, as brushing over contextuality, uniqueness, and the situatedness of any meaningful conceptual claim?

Well, without being able to dive into any details of possible defenses at this point (if such defenses were even necessary after knowing his work more intimately), it may suffice to say that at least the reception of Whitehead's work was complicit in the developing discourses on indigeneity, gender and liberation, as well as interjecting itself into postmodern (poststructuralist) philosophies and postcolonialism. And despite its highly conceptual complexity and claims of metaphysical universality (and despite these characteristics being an additional hindrance to its reception), Whitehead's "organismic" philosophy was not only de facto implemented by, and applied to, many of the current pressing issues facing humanity by diverse disciplines (not only philosophy and theology), but could be (and has been) shown to provide categories by which we might alternatively conceptualize the world as well as create a more human (and humane), peaceful, and diversified civilization of the future. Indeed, Whitehead's work directly or implicitly addresses many of the questions and worries of current relevance: of an ecological future of humanity with this earth; of the peaceful interaction between individuals, societies, and civilizations; of a harmonious collaboration between philosophy, science, and religion; of new and surprising connotations of religious identity and interreligious multiplicity; of a grand cosmological outlook of radical openness with a creative invitation to alternative forms of existence; of explicit instruments for the recognition of power discourses and strategies for a diversion from, and for the overcoming of, power struggles.

In other words, Whitehead's work is, and is recognized by the more sensible observers of the current state of human affairs, as not only relevant for new ways to frame these questions, but providing vital insights offering and addressing alternatives, that is, more peaceful visions of humanity's future (if we survive). This has played out through investments into the application of his suggestions to diverse discourses on ecology, education, economy, race and gender, evolution and society, but also in framing or instigating discourses seeking connections between science, religion, and philosophy, so vital in their accord for the future of humanity. We will dive into several of these areas later, not excluding questions of origins, developments, and current alternatives in Whitehead's reception in these fields. Yet, I want to begin by way of an introduction, to lay out certain parameters for pursuing and preforming process philosophy and theology as they arise from Whitehead's work and as they will set the stage for the deeper layers of the (kind of) introduction that this book is as a whole. I will concentrate on three such parameters or dimensions or contours, here, each of them ever more clearly mapping the field we will walk through in the following chapters, as it helps to situate process theology the way I came to understand it after decades of reflection.

The *First Contour* can be gleaned from the end of Whitehead's last book, *Modes of Thought* (1937), presented to us with a surprising appeal to *the inevitable relationship between society, philosophy, and mysticism*. This triangulation may be established in two steps. First, Whitehead holds that it is one of the most important functions of philosophy to provide society with ever-fresh conceptualizations of reality so as to avoid the petrification of its life into doomed repetitions of its past. One can only imagine how Whitehead's new paradigm of interrelationality and processual connectivity does, indeed, hold us accountable for remaining caught up in a repetition of modes of violence and war, while we *could* escape them by applying new ways to understand the world into which we are born in order to transform ourselves toward nobler aims. In his work on civilization, *Adventures of Ideas* (1933), Whitehead names five: truth, beauty, adventure, art, and peace.

The second connection of this triangulation happens when we ask the question: How can we escape the repetitive prison of the past through a different conceptualization of reality if these are, as evolutionary science and postmodern deconstruction alike (in a surprising synopsis) claim, fundamentally enmeshed in the biological (naturally selected) and cultural (power-inflicted) patterns of knowledge underlying any potential change as inescapable inertia? Whitehead, however, claims that all of our rationalizations of such patterns are not absolutely short-circuited, but actually allow for the participation in the unprecedented, the novel, the unexpected, the unrealized, the imagined. Not unlike the claim of the Buddha that we *can* overcome the causal closedness of karmic repetition, Whitehead names the source of this novelty: mysticism. Yet he defines it—and the process analysis will have to show why this is a feasible claim—as direct insight into depth as yet unspoken. That which is not yet spoken—note the silence beyond, but toward language—is unrealized; even more: it is unthought, uncategorized, but comes into existence through the gift of direct insight or in-sight, internalized vision. That, in order to be able to claim this, one must also posit a resource for the very potentiality of it is evident, and this will be one of the inroads toward Whitehead's spectacular reintroduction of the concept of God into his philosophy. In the context of the triangulation currently under discussion, philosophy appears as rationalization not of the spirit of the time, as philosophy is often tamed looking back on the blunders it produced in its specific cultural settings, but as a spirit of the not yet, the impossible maybe, as Jacques Derrida claims, or the power of the unborn, as the Buddha taught: participation in the event of novelty that cannot be reduced to any past. This rationalization, however, as Whitehead remarks, is not geared toward the elimination of its mysterious character (in some sense being out of the world), but is meant to leave us in (Aristotelian) wonder (rather than Cartesian doubt) at the inexhaustibility of potentials for new social constructions, driving humanization in the direction of deep patterns of harmony and intensity waiting (to use Whitehead's phase from *Process and Reality*) in the womb of nature to be actualized by an awakened (and ever to be awakened) consciousness.

It should be obvious that a theology that is based on such a triangulation is, on the one hand, engaged in the production of concepts that creatively try to pervade social transformation with alternatives to detect means, formulate instruments, and develop visualizations for an ongoing process of reformation toward ideals of truth, beauty, adventure, art, and peace. On the other hand, it withstands the constructivist pitfall of reducing these new patterns to mere expressions of evolutionary algorithms, or mere cultural inventions. Instead, it leaves the mystery of its own enactment an untouched condition and source of renewal. In other words, such a process theology would be "theopolitics" as it cares for a process of "theomorphizing" society, but it recognizes this process to be released from the "theopoetics" of its mystical "indeconstructibility" (to use a term of Derrida's, who reserves it for deconstruction itself *and* the ideal of justice).

The *Second Contour* in which process theology should be nested, on a Whiteheadian basis, is partly tied to the first as one of its formulations appears in the same work, *Modes of Thought,* right after the first one. It is indicated by the inescapable *force field* in which philosophy is to be formulated, namely, that *between poetry and mathematics.* The other similar, although not identical, formulation of this contouration appears in Whitehead's first work after his move to the American continent, also the first one in which he introduces metaphysics formally after limiting himself to matters of philosophy of science, namely, *Science and the Modern World* (1925), with the meaning of a force field *traversing logic and aesthetics.*

Whitehead maintains that philosophy is akin to poetry. This is a controversial claim. Although it was tried out and recurred throughout the history of western philosophy across different philosophical persuasions—from the materialist cosmological poem *De rerum natura* of Lucretius through Nietzsche's postmodern *Zarathustra* to Martin Heidegger's existentialist ruminations on the aphoristic fragments of *Heraclitus* and the poetic work of Hölderlin—it has had its enemies: beginning with Plato's animosity against the poets (they are permanent exiles in his state)—and with them the theological poets, the singers of the divine—to the mathematical inclinations of Spinoza and Leibnitz, and from the rationalism of Descartes to the set-theoretical reconstruction of all reality in the works of Alain Badiou. Whitehead's claim of the poetic nature of philosophical reasoning—and we should be clear that he does herewith claim a poetic ground of rationality as such—can be misunderstood. It does imply, to be sure, that reality on all levels exhibits a fundamental inwardness that cannot be reconstructed by physical externality (some would go on to call this view panpsychism, although Whitehead himself does not), but it does not mean sloppy thinking in the face of the *Anstrengung des Begriffs*, that is, (something like) the effort of conceptualization of Hegel's *Phenomenology of the Spirit* (although even for this work of utter rationalism, Jean Hyppolite could find no better form than a "novel"). Instead, Whitehead relates the nature of this poetics to mathematics since both, in his view, exhibit the search, recognition, and imaginative composition of patterns wherever they may appear or emerge. In another context, Whitehead even envisions mathematics to become much more than it is today or was in the past, namely, not only an instrument of science (and sometimes philosophy), but of cosmological universality as it basically and essentially opens a glimpse into, recognizes, and composes patterns of existence. Here, mathematics remains close to music, and process thought to composition—an image Whitehead uses throughout *Modes of Thought*.

It is in this sense that process theology as theopoetics also exhibits the beauty of theorems of patterns of a divine mind. As far as the world reflects this divine mind and contributes to the ever-new composition of such patterns of beauty in a grand rhythm and harmony and, really (to complete the musical symbolism:), symphony of becoming, it not only forces us to immerse ourselves into the aesthetic nature of its (physical or mental or spiritual) compositions, but inadvertently relates this felt processual wholeness with its own rationality, which is neither lost in mystic abnegation of (especially) physical reality nor engaged in the abandonment of the aesthetic impulse over against bare algorithmic or syllogistic aromatization of (the genesis of) creation.

This is what Whitehead's other formulation of this tension—that between logic and aesthetic—inculcates. And it relates the force field directly to the theological implication: while logic, in Whitehead's cosmological rendering of its relevance, represents an iron law of necessity, aesthetics, without negating logical rationality, underpins it with the grace of the unprecedented, the suggestive and ever-new harmonizations of a process of becoming that is not bound by law, but by love, imagination, and a vision of gentleness. This—and it is Whitehead's twist—can only be represented through at divine reality that neither withholds its suggestiveness of satisfaction beyond any law (be it cosmic or moral), nor delivers us to the grave of logical stringency. It is imaginative, healing, exploring, always turning, seeking the unrealized, and offering unexpected resources of an ever-new (to be composed) future of the cosmic community.

The *Third Contour* appears in Whitehead's only work directly addressing matters of the philosophical conceptualization of religion, namely, *Religion in the Making* (1926), and concerns *the relationship between philosophical cosmology and religion in an evolutionary and multireligious context*. Whitehead cannot only not escape the relevance of religion in his scheme of thought—as his metaphysics wants to embrace all spheres of experience without claims of reductionism or ridicule—but must imply an interface between philosophy and religion or patterns of universal thought and such of unique spiritual experiences (or even revelations). In other words: While process theology is a philosophical theology—the aesthetic side of cosmology, as it were—it allows, because of this theopoetic underpinning, modes of self-revelation, that is, modes of religious exquisiteness in the midst of logical generalities.

Here, process theology becomes fundamentally (as I call it) "transreligious," that is, allowing (only) for a pluralistic accommodation of the aesthetic uniqueness of religious experiences in a metaphysical framework of patterns of existence—as this framework is (or will always be) already enveloped by the multiply folded aesthetic reality. It is in this sense that process theology transgresses not only the boundary between modes of thought and explorations of reality (such as science, philosophy, and religion), but also their underlying presuppositions, especially the seeming mutual exclusion of inclusive unity and exceptional uniqueness of modes of existence, thought and values, persons and societies, nature and culture, physicality and spiritual realities.

This proposed manifold of process theology, enwrapped by, and released through, aesthetic interrelationality, will therefore, whether this would be historically true or not, be bound by any locality in which process theology might have had it origin, such as a specific philosophical or religious tradition, or embededness in any metanarrative, such as the Occident over against the Orient or the North over against the (global) South. In fact, not only is Whitehead aware of the limitation his thought exhibits because of such localizations, he embraces such limitations in a perhaps different sense than we might expect: not only as an epistemic humbleness regarding one's roots and restraints, but as the cauldron for the creation of value and, hence, meaning at all. This means these limitations are not conductive of tribalistic isolation or minority reports (to avoid submission or dissolution in imperial majority cultures), at least not primarily, but of creative conditions of meaning to be communicated and connected to the multiplicity of alterations and alternatives as they arise in the same or between different cultural contexts. Contextuality is not a debilitating hindrance to, but an empowerment of, mutual community. Hence, Whitehead warns that his philosophy does not accept the divide of rationalism and empiricism of western philosophy, or even the dichotomy of western over against Indian and Chinese thought pattern; and also: Whitehead's philosophy is rather at the preface of the split between the continental and analytic philosophical empires than an expression of it. Consequently, Whitehead did not see his Christian upbringing as a limitation when exposing his philosophy to the question of the evolution and meaning of religions, and any religious experience, really, as well as their conceptualizations. In fact, he recognized eastern religions, especially Buddhism, as genuine as western ones; and although he never stopped using the notion of God, he confessed that he did mean something that cuts across western personal and eastern hyper-personal categorizations of ultimate reality.

It is in this context that I feel comfortable to develop Whitehead's thought and, hence, process theology not only within and as an expression of a limited western philosophy: one metaphysical in nature instead of phenomenological, neither clearly continental nor analytical enough, nor poststructuralist enough, while not being fit to contribute to either pragmatism or the English idealism of his time. Rather, I see his thought in general and process theology in particular as trangressional modes of communication between, and communion of, these forms of western philosophy and some important eastern philosophical patterns (which have their own history within process theology). I also feel comfortable not to limit Whitehead to western religious expressions of thought or experience, but to understand his philosophical creations conductive of, and congeniously expressing, many diverse religious traditions at once precisely since they embraces the contrast between eastern and western patterns of thought and experience.

To recapitulate: Mediated through, and motivated by, these Three Contours of Whiteheadian thought expressed in this preamble, and because they can function as a basis for the understanding and categorization of process thought, I will lead you through *Five Spheres* of its interlocked perspectives, be they more philosophical or more situated in religious discourse. The tunes of these spheres (like intonations of a spherical instrument), as it were, will be shot through by themes welling from the intimate connections I see between Whitehead's thought and, for instance, poststructuralist philosophy, but also transreligious intimations of unique experiences, which, in Whitehead's view, meant to express the finest unique moments of metaphysical universality. These Spheres are mutually enhancing, but independent enough to be accessed in any order to which the reader might be inclined. Every of the five parts will first introduce the Sphere of thought followed by *Sixteen Explorations*, distributed among the Spheres, highlighting some of their respective implications, but also mutually connecting elements discussed throughout other Spheres. They can be read after the series of Spheres as series for themselves or in their integrity with their respective Spheres or whenever any of the Explorations touch on themes in a Sphere. In the end, I will come back to compress the thought patterns as a whole in *Three Contours Of Becoming* mirroring the Three Contours To Come with which all began.

SPHERE I

THE COMMUNITY OF BECOMING

THIS FIRST SPHERE IS concerned with Whitehead's work insofar as it has provided the basis for, and remains the context of, an adequate understanding of the sources and major themes of process theology. What is more, by way of this "situatedness," one can demonstrate the (reasons for the) perpetual embededness of process theology in Whitehead's new philosophical approach, because it opens up for us a whole new world, as it were, the fascination of and the engagement with which never left the creative developments that became known as process theology. Hence, many of the motifs and conceptual decisions imprinted in the specific outlook of process theologies—to which we will turn later in the book—can be readily perceived in the way they developed from this "new world(view)."

During his career, Whitehead was never only the mathematician or philosopher of science or metaphysician, but was also eminently engaged in matters of education. This is not least attested to by his collected writings *Aims of Education* (1929). It finds its nucleus in the paper of the same name, originally given as presidential address to the Mathematical Association of England in 1916. Whitehead promoted an education system that would play to the creative resources of every learner; would situate educational methods not in the context of rigid repetition of traditions as facilitated by the industrialization of learning and the mechanization of sedimented standards, which was only functionalizing education for economic efficiency; and would propose an effort against any specialization that would undercut the creative exchange of the learner with knowledge and experience. Furthermore, Whitehead forcefully (and successfully) argued for the accessibility of the patriarchal, closed academic echelon of the higher education system to women. And he rallied for the foundational importance of democratic values in the educational process and beyond. He understood his endeavor to emphasize the development of the ability of "thinking (on your own)" as most important impulse for any communal probing of potentials for a different society of the future.

This "poetic" instead of mechanical impetus found visible expression especially in his book *Adventures of Ideas*, which could be interpreted as his analysis, diagnosis, prescription, and encouragement of (new) modes of thought for the development of civilizations. Seeking out (new) motivations for individual and collective forms of human self-transcendence, which were gathering around such grand ideals as truth, beauty, art, adventure, and peace, are, for Whitehead not in the least aberrant features of baseless projection (of a dreamer), but are deeply consonant with his philosophical convictions, his metaphysical and cosmological insights, and the structural features of his new organismic outlook or worldview or, maybe even better: his envisioning and philosophical formulation of a newly found experience of (everything) being in a common world.

Symptomatic, or rather symbolic, for this integrity of thought for, and practical anticipation of, a transformed civilization of the future is a conversation Whitehead had at his home at Harvard with Charles Lindbergh in the late 1930s. While discussing, among other things, the world political situation, and in tending their attention to the future of humanity, Whitehead, against the turmoil of the past and present wars' political and humanitarian havocs, ventured in a surprising direction. He articulated the firm hopes for the survival of humanity and a future for the next hundreds of years *if* it was able to tap into, and (in its potential maturity) was able to implement, the forces of gentleness over and against the all-present, seeming inability to escape or consciously let go of the powers of destruction. This statement will only seem to be ironic at that time if we forget that Whitehead also systematically thought that divine engagement in the cosmos and throughout human development is always (and only) acting through the tender elements in the world, which slowly and in quietness operate by love. As we will see, this does not suggest an idealistic or unrealistic flight beyond the facts (already clothed in a pessimistic view of the abilities of human nature or the human condition), but deeply reflects Whitehead's understanding of the mutual indwelling of facts and values such that the imaginative and bold realization of the latter is what the facts of the future *can* be(come).

More specifically, the ability and supposed potential for a mature transformation of the human condition in individual and communal contexts (which in Whitehead's philosophical outlook are themselves inextricably intertwined) are accorded to the *cosmically* (and hence humanly) inherent values of with, in Whitehead's vision, truth, beauty, art, adventure, and peace are the most profound. The highlighting of such patterns of existence is, therefore, the expression rather than the exception of an organic view of universal entanglement to which humanity is continuous. And since humanity is emergent from the body of cosmic interrelatedness in a process that even entangles divine suggestions of such a "virtuous" development, we will not go wrong to understand the scope of Whitehead's thought and hope for the transformation toward a new society that patterns itself after these values as deeply ecological in nature. The whole universe (and beyond that *any* universe) is a vast, complex, moving whole shot through with the realization of values the creative or destructive outcomes of which has created its past and will effectuate its very future. At the deepest layer of existence as such, the world is a community of becoming.

In hindsight, we can realize that the tendency of widening the scope of reference in Whitehead's work over time to universal categories of a cosmological and metaphysical nature was interwoven with the fundamental insight with which any specific (philosophical) understanding must correlate: the profound recognition of the deeply ecological nature and structure of the universe. This insight may be seen as the motive force that was about to be unveiled in his writings: from the early mathematical writings, especially his *Universal Algebra* (1898), which set the tone with its interest in all forms that patterns of interrelated multiplicities can take, to his applied physical mathematics, which asked the question of ultimate material entities and found them in relational intersections of fields; from his (and Bertrand Russell's) enterprise of deducing mathematics from logics in *Principia Mathematica* (1905), which, while creating symbolic logic and becoming the basis for analytic philosophy, failed, as Whitehead foresaw and Kurt Gödel (with his Incompleteness Theorem) proved, to his books *Principles of Natural Knowledge* (1919) and *The Concept of Nature* (1920), in which Whitehead explored the relational event character of the physical universe while also detecting the fundamental incoherence of this picture as long as it splits the world into mind and matter; from the recognition of modern post-mechanistic, relativistic, and probabilistic physics in *Principles of Relativity* (1922) and its relevance for the development of an organic view of the universe, the introduction of metaphysics and the (still developing) notion of God in *Science of the Modern World* (1925) to a related reflection on Religion in *Religion in the Making* (1926); from the fully developed philosophical cosmology and "natural theology" of the opus magnum *Process and Reality* (1929) to the turn to its implications for civilization in *Adventures of Ideas* (1933); finally, from the recognition of the integration of the life of matter with that of the mind in *Modes of Thought* (1937) to the last writings on "Mathematics and the Good" and "Immortality" (1941) in which the impossible, the processual unity of all opposites, even that of mathematics and the Good and that of impermanence and immortality, is confirmed in truly late words of wisdom.

Yet, the most daring aspect of these ever-wider horizons of thinking may be found more hidden as a twofold complexity in unique Whiteheadian intertwining emerges, especially in the two smaller, but visionary books *Symbolism* (1927) and *The Function of Reason* (1929)—written around and between Whitehead's more commonly known and celebrated books. On the one hand, we begin to realize that, in Whitehead's analysis, the widest horizon of thought is not that of metaphysical universality, but of the civilizational dynamics implicating a metaphysical consciousness. That is, the ultimate horizon of philosophy is not static abstraction of what (maybe) *is* (out there), but actualization of what *could be* in a process of universally entangled *becoming*. On the other hand, it is not the breadth of universalization that ultimately counts, but a venturing into the *depth* of this becoming in which its very evolution contributes to ever deeper levels of experience ultimately emerging as depth of mind and spirit. The community of becoming reaches its true depth when it begins to recognize that which it has harbored all along: when it begins to venture into the realization of potentials far beyond the sleep of dull matter and awakens to (a civilization of) universal solidarity with the feeling, striving, and loving *cosmos*, integrating itself into its eco-nature, but also elevating its ecological origins into a vision always anticipatory of unprecedented beauty and peace.

It is in this context, that is, the civilizational integration of metaphysical conceptions, that Whitehead's rigorous exploration of the relevance of religion and a serious reflection from within it as well as on it in its importance for the emergence of a peaceful civilization of the future becomes significant. It is this reflection on civilization and religion that forms the context in which Whitehead can collect the necessary conceptual resources—within and beyond metaphysical considerations (that began at the same time to dominate his work)—that will issue in the formulation of his mature and unique concept of God. And one can say with confidence that it is this Whiteheadian notion of God with its specific conceptual connotations that has become (whether affirmed, revisioned, or rejected) the signature under any legitimate conception worth connoting the name of process theology.

Moreover, it is precisely this process concept of God that expresses and signals the effort to formulate a new and fresh, but equally venerable, paradigm in which all philosophical and theological categories, which it would allow us to develop, become expressive of a comprehensive vision of unity in diversity: the unity in diversity of God and the world; the unity in diversity of humanity, culture, and nature; the unity in diversity of creation and salvation; the unity in diversity of science, philosophy, and religion; the unity in diversity of all with all in all. Whitehead effectuates this unity in diversity by way of two simultaneous conceptual strategies: relationality and process. Relationality signifies the inescapable "place" of the gathering of everything, the all, in the actualization of its inherent potentialities. Like Plato before and Derrida after him, Whitehead calls this "place" (which is a translation of the Greek term) *khora,* to which we will come back later. Process, again, signalizes that this gathering or togetherness is only made possible by a *becoming* of relations. Both together comprise the deeper meaning of space and time, not (only) as physical constructs (as which they are already abstractions), but as ingredients of occasions of actuality, that is, of acts of reality (in their activity of real-izing reality) that, in the multiplicity of their actual effects, span the space of the relations of all to all in every moment of becoming and keep it in its processual movement.

It may be also noted at this point that it is in recognizing these deeper layers of reality—the realization of relations in process—that we have taken the first step in following the Whiteheadian movement from the physical reality of facts, such as space and time (and matter or energy), to their reconstruction as abstractions from the processual relationality of existence. That these include and exhibit movements and structures of value or consist of a unity in diversity of processes of valuation will only become more intelligible when we dive further into the inner workings of this relational process as that of happenings of related *events* of their actualization—a universe (consisting) of actual occasions or actual entities of such happenings.

Given the paradigmatic form that "unity in diversity" takes in Whitehead's thought, we can also say that it indicates itself to be a relational process in which all oppositions, which we might perceive of it, but rather construct so as to understand this world, in some way coincide. Or conversely, one could say: these oppositions only appear as mutually exclusive or obstructive contrariness (in our mind) insofar as they are (its) mental abstractions. Yet, in reality—so Whitehead—it is in this moving whole of actual reality that matter and mind concur (without ever having been separated in the first place) and depart again from one another in every moment of happening—Whitehead calls it a (microscopic) "epoch"—of this (macrocosmic) cosmic space of time—Whitehead calls this a "cosmic epoch"—so as to suffer new adventures. In the mutual community of the all of these events, unimagined worlds realize themselves and the deeper sense of existence fulfills itself, namely: the ever novel, yet ever more abundant realization of a gestalt of world as a community of all creatures/creations, which by diverse religions and their scriptural witnesses was understood as the coming (advent) of a realm of peace—be it in this world or another. At this point, it will suffice to point to the fact that this approach also houses not only social, but also deep ecological and ethical implications.

If we ask for the reason why Whitehead is not attempting to appropriate any (if only implicit) form of the Cartesian dualism of mind and matter, but why he, instead, understands such a conceptualization an abstractions of the world-ordering human mind, we will discover that Whitehead bears an elementary and irrevocable resistance against the view that we could trust any kind of reductionism to generate an intelligible account of the relational events of becoming. Otherwise, the web of the space-time of the cosmos would unravel again into unrelated and unintelligible models of either atomic splinters or an indifferentially fused mesh, not compatible with the experience of the world as, at the same time, processual and structured cosmos. For this and any kind of reductionism, emphasizing one side of a pair of opposites would fall on the side of either unity or diversity. What such a reductionism would make us believe in is, however, (even if only tacitly) always already built on such a Cartesian dualism. This holds true whether it appears in the scientific materialism of the nineteenth century that, for Whitehead, was led ad absurdum by a philosophy such as the one that developed by drawing on the witness of the new, revolutionary physics of the early twentieth century. And it applies equally to any form of spiritual reductionism, which tries to completely ablate the meaning of the world into a sphere of a purely spiritual (realm of) divinity. As such a philosophy or, better, worldview strives that leaves a universe of matter and energy, space and time, but more generally, of finiteness, behind by filling our hopes with promises of an afterworld, it also abandons experienced reality for a dream world that is supposedly innocent of all of these categories of finiteness and impermanence.

What implication does this have for articulating a theological or divine dimension of the experience of the universe? The shortest way to answer this question at this point is maybe this: In Whitehead's account of unity in diversity (holding together all perceived opposites), God and the world, are the most universal symbols of the (meaning of) relational processiality that is reality. Without negating the abstract character of such formulations, but harboring their concrete meaning, they represent not irreconcilable realities or components of a categorical error (as if one reality can be captured by pointing at the other), but they appear *categorically* as abstracted moments of *one* universal relational process. The maybe shortest formulation to indicate this most universal unity in diversity of reality as a whole, then, is this: God and the world are, in this view, to be understood as constants of reciprocal becoming, as a community of mutual inspiration to ever new futures and ever new adventures that find their existence and justification in the (potentially "happy") actualization ("happening") of intensity and harmony.

Note that it is not categorical oppositions that carry the meaning of their reality, but a process in which they (and their categorical articulation) are tied by ever newly emerging contrasts. Hence, neither is God only spirit (or mind, for that matter), infinity, an unimpressed omnipotent sublime being, or only a transcendent horizon, nor is the world in the multiplicity of its events of happening only matter, energy, space-time, finitude, or a merely immanent existent. Although never a matter of identity or mixture, between these realities prevails neither an alienation nor a foreignness that would not already be enveloped by, and grounded in, the relational community of their mutual becoming. It is in this sense that Whitehead comprehends every event of world, that is, every actual occasion of happening, as conceptual (mental, transcendental) and corporeal (physical, immanent) unity in the multiplicity of becoming (of world). He calls this unity in diversity the polarity of mental and physical pole. Every actual occasion of the world is an actualization of reality in the realization of which it collects its (unimaginable wide and deep) past in its own multiplicity and contradictoriness in such a way that will allow it to release itself again into a new, unknown future within its own transcendental horizon of novelty. Through this inner transformation (from past to future, from matter to mind, from immanence to transcendence, and vice versa), this process is constrained, but not totally determined. Every event leaves more or less harmony and intensity behind (in the physical world) and, hence, increases or decreases the world by its (transcendent) self-realization. And it is the internal (transcendental) quality of the (immanent) intensity of becoming—and no event exhibits only external (material) qualities—by which world events either begin to mirror (more) the divine intention for (cosmic) unity of diversity or contribute to the darkening of the continence of the divine Wisdom, which is always pursuing its increased realization in any event.

In the immanent transcendence of every event of happening in and from any other—as it is performed in the sense of contrasts of past and future, continuity and novelty, freedom and fate, mind and matter, potentiality and actualization, intensity and harmony—is to be found the prefiguration for the archetype, a divine reality in which all contrasts are (perfectly) united in a most sublime manner, or conversely: through the reality, that is, realization of which all contrasts unfold as relational process of unification in diversification in the world. Only through this—in Whitehead's terminology—"incarnation" of God in the world in every of its happenings as a network of relations in becoming is the world saved from mere externality (materiality), that is, from being dammed to disappear in a mere chaos of bagatelles drowning in mere ir-reality (un-realization). Instead, through the presence of a divine initiation of every happening *and* a gentle acceptance of the (in whatever sense) insufficient realizations of its potentials, the world (in every of its events) appears *as* world: as cosmos, as beautiful orderedness, as contrast between being and becoming, which even in its tragic side of the process of becoming and perishing is, and can be experienced as, embraced by a meaning that expresses itself already in the such-ness (Buddhists would say: *tathata*) of the mere existence of *such* ordered, *such* communicating, *such* becoming, *such* ever novel, *such* infinitely manifold world movements. The wonder of existence, for Whitehead, is less the one of being and nothingness, *that* something is, but rather the wonder that something can only (come to) be because it is in *such* a way: communicative, relational, becoming, realizing itself in the often incomprehensible, mysterious, and (against all failures and downfalls) awe-inspiring unfolding of harmonies and intensities of becoming. Such intuitions of the abundance of relationship and the dynamics of realization are irreducibly ultimate in Whitehead's thought. And even the little categories, by which we try to capture the world, as they might wish to ignore, or may be misled by their inner logic to despise, such deep intuitions (by imagining to escape prematurely the fragile implications of a world of becoming and perishing or to reduce themselves to the mere external side of it) have such intuitions already as their performative precondition, namely, as the very patterns of experience.

All being (or the being of the all) has a (or is in) becoming; from nothingness nothing becomes. These Whiteheadian maxims (which really go back to the earliest, historically available occidental and oriental witnesses of philosophical thought and religious intuition) are the inherent outcome of a mode of thought in which the *feeling* (in the fullness of what experience can mean, which Whitehead will name "prehension") of the world marks the concreteness of any realization of being and becoming. Such a feeling (individually and collectively) is, as an inherent process of the creative gathering of relations beyond itself, best understood as an *aesthetic* unity in diversity (or better: as an aesthetic process of unification and diversification). As such an aesthetic process, not only is any process described as an event of/as feeling (experience), but also already—given the divine initiation and perception—as an urgent instance of decision (or as theologians would say: a *kairos*) that as such always releases or lessens the continence of divine operation into the world's further becoming. But it also already magnifies and releases into consciousness every event to be (or become as) a mode of spiritual perception, thereby revealing the gravities of it having a unique meaning for itself, the world, and God. Here, we encounter Whitehead's God. God is not to be constructed in the image of a cosmocrat on whom all control would be incumbent (as if control was the highest value of a relational world in becoming). Nor does God indicate a reality that is aloof above the world (first of all concerned with itself in itself). Nor are we asked to follow such motivations of religious activity that would seek divine reality against all else, because we feel to be completely expendable and, hence, conclude that it would be better to desire and seek the security of a rock in the surf of becoming. Such a God would denigrate the world of becoming as undesirable, at best as means for the judgment of our behavior, but otherwise dispensable (and finally dispensed of)—unfortunately, a very common theological worldview exhibiting all essential marks of the dualistic reductionism against which Whitehead was revolting. Rather, God stands for that reality (the process of relational realization) that *unfolds* itself in its realization (the becoming real in its real effects of actualization) by capacitating everything to become a living tension between past realizations and new intensities, novelties, and harmonies of the future. And, at the same time, it *enfolds* everything in its actual becoming (the realization of itself) as it weaves this manifold into ever-new unifications. These unifications (in diversification) carry the complex coincidence of opposite movements of thought, which are in reality also one: they mean processes of a healing gathering into Godself *and* processes of a wholesome inweaving of this saved reality of every event with the world of new becoming. Divine reality is engaged in every process of becoming (without ever substituting it) by initiating it and delivering it to itself, but also by accompany them in order to elevate them again (in) to itself.

If God, in this spiritual paradigm, does not appear to ever be without a world, neither the world without God, this should not be constructed as the making of an insufficient God (violating the sovereignty of God), but as a new, wider, living, and deeper understanding of God's supreme relationality and a sufficiency that can tolerate, instigate, and even love becoming. If God was always already incarnated in everything, even as the world is interwoven with, and perceived into, God, this should not be construed as a loss of divine eternity and even divinity, but should be understood as the supreme becoming of a God who can suffer and integrate (and even consist of supreme) processuality, of event-living spirit. If there is nothing that could exist without the luxurious abundance of relationships, nor succeed (or fail) without the dynamics of living becoming, this must not be construed as deficiency of divine completeness, but should be understood as a completeness or perfection that is never in the past tense perfect; rather, it encompasses the perfections of unsurpassable becoming and a completeness that lives from relationality.

It is here that it becomes obvious that what might appear as a defect, is really based on perception; but the superficiality of this perception can only be recognized as such if we follow the new and fascinating worldview Whitehead tempt us to imagine: to try a deeper sounding of our experiential reality instead of clinging to the reductionist, dualist, and power-laden sedimentations of a patriarchal ideology of control and domination reigning over this perception. For Whitehead and process theology, this revolution in the construction of new philosophical and theological categories arises from the very patterns inherent in experiences itself. As this experience unveils itself as fundamentally poetic instead of mechanic in nature, it presents itself as nothing less than a sign of the wonder of existence itself, open to everyone (and in a true sense, everything) *if* we are willing to open our outer and inner eyes and ears to its feeling.

So, as process theology talks about the world as a community in/of becoming, it does so from the deep structures of experience. And if it understands God in terms of becoming, it trusts the deep intuitions of experience to exhibit, prepare for, receive, and comprehend its own deepest reality to be a gift of divine becoming: the divine ability to release events into their own existence and self and the capacity to receive novelty from the adventure of the world. If God, in Whitehead's thought, appears to be couched in categories of becoming, this must, *then*, also not be disavowed as unfortunate loss of the (only) legitimate concept of the reality of "God" (who is, thereby, still defined from the all-important character of omnipotence). Rather, the transformation of thought, feeling, and living, which prepares for, comprises, and initiates this spiritual turn, can now be understood to mark a contemporary, matured reconstruction of the wealth of our human heritage of spiritual experiences, mystical insights, and philosophical as well as theological efforts, or better: of their reclamation or proclamation. And such a proclamation would, indeed, resonate with the intention of a manifold of scriptural accounts of a multiplicity of religions and spiritual communities as they gather themselves in their identity around such thoughts, experiences, and insights like revelations of ultimate concern. Their paradigm has never been and now again ceased to be a scheme of thought in which *power* would stand for divine reality, but rather *love;* a love that does not know of violence, only of a potentiality that capacitates and releases; a love even that would not want to be without such an interwoven community.

This conception of the world and its reverse side, its congenial conception of God, are not based on flight or fear that would need to make headway and form a bulwark against the fragility of the world; it would not stand in need of any immunization against becoming and perishing; and it would not need to call for an apocalyptic overcoming of the transient world. Conversely, rather following Buddhist paths, it accepts the impermanence of the all as profound. And it agrees with the admonitions of diverse religions to overcome the fearful self as the incurvated paradigm of meaninglessness. Thereby, such reconceptualization of God and the world (and their relationship) renders the Whiteheadian reflection all the more urgent and, as a contrast model, inevitable. Especially in the contemporary climate in which humanity as a whole demonstrates its inability to weave truth and freedom into patterns of a peaceful society and to recognize itself as a cosmic community with all creatures, process theology—should we bring ourselves to say that it has an essence (a unity in diversity)—is meant to be this exigent thinking. Its imperative is that of a love—therein following the love of God—in a fragile world that calls for a realization of its potentials to disavow the drama of its violation, that is, the subsumption of relationship and becoming under the shadow of violence and overpowering. Insofar as process theology unravels the motives of the generation of this drama, its sympathy of non-violence in theory and praxis wants to invite us to let go of, and to let fade away, the tragic effects of this drama into the oblivion of the past, even as we could envision new and unchartered futures beyond its limitations.

Exploration 1

THE EVENT

IT IS ALWAYS ONE of the most difficult questions how to gain access to one of the fundamental conceptual spheres of Whitehead's thought par excellence, namely that of the event. For a deeper understanding, it is important to notice that Whitehead uses different terms with different inner workings and scopes to address this reality of the event—in fact, in some ways the most concrete reality in Whitehead's philosophy. In Whitehead's earlier works, for instance, *The Concept of Nature*, the term *event* indicates the ultimate irreducibility of a certain thickness of space-time with a certain character of which mathematical dimensionless entities, such as points, are mere abstractions. He calls their happening "the creative passage of nature." In later works, he differentiates between events and actual occasions or entities. While actual occasions are drops of experience— actualities in becoming, unifications of relations, becoming and perishing, self-creative and momentary—events become understood as series of actual occasions insofar as they do not instantiate any perpetual character, but still are related to one another in some defined way. Whitehead also differentiates actual occasions from actual entities insofar as all concrete actualities of becoming are actual entities, while God, since God is not a momentary drop of perishing experience, is not an actual occasion. However, even by risking fuzziness, I will generally go on to speak of the intended reality as event—since even Whitehead often transgressed his own definitions so as to not lose the vividness of the reality he wanted to reveal in his terminology (instead of fixating a dogmatic dictionary of definitions, which Whitehead explicitly refuted).

Another set of differentiations is required here before I will try to exemplify the reality behind the event. The reality of the event must be differentiated from *nexuses* of events, that is, either a temporal or spatial series of events as they relate to one another in mutual perception (prehension) of their becoming; and they are the basis of *societies* of events, that is, structured and in some way permanent organisms in the multiplicity and variety of which the universe is populated. I will come back to these higher-grade concrete realities later (Exploration 2). Although events (actual entities), nexuses, and societies are all in their own way exemplifications of the concrete realities in existence—which implies that they cannot be further reduced to anything else, to one another, or to any more concrete realities—events are the most ultimate components of actual reality, and any concert actuality is precisely not abstract, because it exists only "in becoming."

While, most of the time, it is presupposed (although this is not shared by all interpreters of Whitehead) that actual entities are microscopic in nature and in space-time extension (they create space-time when they have become), my example will deliberately choose something we can all experience in our everyday life: a car accident. Whitehead can do so too when he, for instance, directs our attention to a moment of our present consciousness—as it moves from now to now, inheriting the past moment of consciousness as object of the experience of the present moment of subjective becoming and in anticipation of future potential developments of their content. But I wanted to escape the potential danger of the image of events being confined to the purely subjective introspection. Given that Whitehead also could on occasion speak of a "super-actuality" (the unity of a nexus in an event and counted as an actual occasion), I rather risk integrating a multiplicity of actual occasions in a macroscopic event (blurring the more technical division between occasions and nexuses). Another way to escape this restriction would be to take the physical path of exemplification as it appears, for instance, in Whitehead's example of an electron as consisting of a whole burst of occasions bound by a permanent character, which seems to us like a thing, a being that "is" instead of a nexus of becoming and perishing occasions. Instead, I will use a car accident to explore in a more diffused, but hopefully intuitive way some vital elements of the strange reality of the event of which Whitehead thinks all that is (as far as it is not an abstraction) consists.

Consider a car accident (and we will replay it several times to emphasize the different aspects): as you drive towards an intersection, you realize that another car enters it from another side. With this realization you hit the brakes, while you see both cars slide into one another. In the very moments since you (and maybe also the other driver) became aware of the situation, your consciousness perceives and follows the movements of both cars toward one another. And with a mixture of the feeling of fate that you will not be able to avoid the crash, but maybe also a slight hope that you may be able to avoid a crash and just slide by the other car, you wait as the event of the accident unfolds . . . does it happen or not? Did it happen or not? Let's rehearse some of the implications constituting this event.

Here is a first analysis. As long as the car accident is happening, it has not happened yet. In other words: as long as the process of its becoming is in progress, it is not yet a car accident. Instead, there is still the hope or fear that it might (not) happen. This is the first important insight. An event "is not" (does not exist) as long as it happens (becomes). When it has happened, it "is," but, at the same time, it "is not" anymore, that is, it has ceased to become. The "reality" of an event demonstrates a profound paradox: its reality of becoming does not exist as fact as long as it is actually happening; its facticity presupposes that its becoming has passed. As long as an event "exists," it does not yet exist; but when it finally exists, it does not "exist" anymore. In reality, an event never exists (in the world of facts); but without its "nonexistence" (becoming), no facts would have comes into existence either. Or as I say: an event does not exist, but it *in-sists*. The event (as it happens) in-sists only in its interior becoming, not as objective fact. But it has also an objective side, an "ex-sistence" beyond itself (beyond its becoming). This is the reason that Whitehead, in *Adventures of Ideas*, ruminates with Plato that "nonbeing" has also a being (namely that of the past). And we might add: that "being" (becoming) is also a form of "nonbeing."

Another important feature of the car accident becomes available when we shift our perspective from the present as future to the past axis to that of the past as future in the present. When the car accident has or has not happened, at a certain point, we know whether it was or was not a car accident. At this point, we might think how we got there.

What if I had only seen the other car a moment earlier (so that this would not have happened)? What if I would have seen it a moment later (so that it would have happened)? What if I would not have taken this street (as I normally avoid it)? What if I would not have woken up a minute late (because I forgot to set the alarm clock, or because I got home too late, or because I had a strenuous day before)?

What we gain from this second analysis are five further characteristics unique to the reality of events: first, an event is surrounded by, and immersed in, a cloud of potentialities, of different outcomes, of possibilities and alternatives, which disappear, are realized, are excluded, are determined as soon as the event can be named as a fact—*this* event, not another one. Whitehead differentiates these possibilities into two categories: *real* possibilities or potentials, insofar as they represent to be expected alternative outcomes of an event, given its past, and the past of all of its elements: my wakefulness after a long day yesterday allows for the alternative of being effective or not; the condition of my brakes could be good or bad; the street could be slippery or not; and so on. Their coming together in this event is undetermined as long as their play is happening, which *is* the event. But all of these potentials are related to realistic influences of the past (although undetermined by their togetherness in this event). *Pure* possibilities, on the other hand, are merely possible, but without either a foothold in the past (the real forces entering in the event) or beyond expected range of options of an event. That the brakes' maintenance could be good or bad might have a real influence on the final outcome of this event; that it does not brake at all, is a slight, but still real potential of the situation; but that there is suddenly no brake there when I hit it, seems to be a mere possibility (of another, imaginary world maybe). Finally, there are *impossibilities*. They also relate to both groups of possibilities, that is, they limit the field of the possible and potential for any event; the restraint the sphere of the event. That I was not even there when this event happened to me is a logical impossibility and hence limits (if one can say so) the field of the pure possibilities related to this (and any) event. That an earthquake on the other side of the world that happened just a minute before the potential car accident has contributed to the event is a restraint on the real potentials since it cannot per physical law (the limited speed of causal influences) have become part of this event.

Second, the event is determined by its specific decisions among these potentials. Such decisions do not have to be a sign of the presence of a subjective mind, but they indicate a reality that is mental rather than physical (think of quantum probabilities) and in any case a determination among potentials and possibilities. This is the reason that Whitehead calls the essence of actuality—the only reality that is concrete (in its actual happening before it becomes a fact)—"decision": the cutting away of potentials in a process of determination of a concrete fact. Although this process does not need to be a subject deciding, here, the potential of such a reality comes into view. And although this process does not need to indicate change, permanence is only the repetition of the same decisions, like a habit, a character. And it has another implication: events are valuation processes. That is, any decision creates an order of potential influences and outcomes of greater or lesser relevance to this event. That the Eifel Tower could in some way have contributed to the car accident, even if it happened in Vienna, not in Paris, is a real possibility, but a really faint one, that is, it is definitely only of low value for its determination. But that the light of the sun has blinded me just when the other car entered into the intersection so that I might have otherwise seen the car a moment earlier, is of high importance for the determination of this event. And again, although this "ordering" of potentials and possibilities regarding their relevance for this particular event is neither necessarily absolutely predetermined (a rigged or forced event) nor subjectively decided (an aesthetic event), yet as soon as we can speak of subjectivity being involved in the event, valuation is a matter of course for its happening.

Third, every event is unique—in its becoming and as a fact (when it has become). You cannot go to court and claim reparations for just any car accident different from yours, one in which you were not involved. In fact, contrary to "substances"—understood as persisting throughout time independently from characteristic changes (a blue hat that changes into a red hat is still a hat)—events must claim all of its elements as having come together in a unique combination that can differ in nothing, nothing at all, without being (identifiable) as a different event. Moreover, it is the existence of the fact of this past event that persists as such with all of its ingredients, being bound by its place and time in the continuum. It is so unique that it cannot be shifted; it has become fixed in the matrix of the world, forever located in its particular past. Or as I say: its in-sistence in itself has become insistence on other events—uniqueness upon uniqueness—as it was the insistence of the events of its own past that it included in its own in-sistence (Exploration 14). This has two further implications: The creative process of any event always has two sides: one of "concrescence" (self-becoming from other events in the past of this event, or *becoming*) and one of "transition" (being part of the becoming of other events, or *being*). Since Whitehead does not think that there can be future events (in the sense of actual entities or occasions), events have two tenses of their existence (insistence) and a cloud of potentials as their future. The other implication here is also of great importance: that events do "become," but they do *not* "change." As facts, they rather indicate unique space-time characters or historical facts, as it were. This will be important to understand the claim of process theology (so feared by classical metaphysicians and considered a danger by religious orthodoxies building or justifying themselves on them) that God "becomes," instead of which one uninformed of this difference often hears (and fears): God "changes."

Fourth, as much as events are determined toward their future (as facts in other events), they are in some way indetermined toward their past. When did the car accident begin? When I saw the other car? When I hit the brakes? When I began to fear or hope and closed my eyes in expectation? When I took the unusual street? When I woke up late? When I had a difficult day yesterday? There is no clear-cut definition of causes that contributed or did not contribute to this (and any) event. In other words: everything that possibly could have contributed to it, that which is in the past of the event the way it was, in fact, appears as a fact of its past and contributed in some way to its becoming. The whole world, as it was factually the past of this specific event, is somehow its cause. Whitehead calls this the "actual world" of an event. It is a perspective of the whole of the world and the whole of the universe in this perspective. This has two further implications: no world of any event embraces all the world there is (except there was only one event, but that event would not have a world). Hence, there are always many worlds of events, some of them will intersect, some of them will not. This again implies that there are events that do not and cannot influence one another insofar as their worlds are not congruent, that is, they include elements of influence that are excluded from the other event's world. This is of course a matter of time: the further back in time one goes from a particular event, the more it becomes likely that the world of one event would intersect with another event's world, or universe. Since the sphere of an actual world shrinks the closer we come to the present of the event, evermore events will not share in the immediate past of one another. Hence, contemporary events will be *independent* from another. Whitehead speaks of the "irresponsibility" of the spatially contemporary events and an "elbow freedom" in the universe: spatiality and indeterminacy condition one another in Whitehead's universe of events.

In recapitulating the features of events, we can say that they are "experiences" in the structure of "prehensions"; that they are present realities sui generis more fundamental than things or substances; that they exhibit more than potentials and facts, namely feelings and forms of feelings; and that they are instances of self-creativity. Events are experiences, that is, they are not theories or abstractions of any kind (although these are included in events as its potentials); rather they are actual because they are experienced—by their own constitution as "in-sistent" gatherings of other experiences (concrescence) and their (the other events') "insistence" in them (transition), but also, conversely, by their "insistence" in other "in-sistences" beyond themselves. Moreover, experiences exhibit not only this "external" (macroscopic, nexic) duality, but also an "internal" (microscopic, atomic) one by gathering themselves always through two poles, the "physical pole" of their past and the "mental pole" of their cloud of potentials open for decision. Implicitly, therefore, each event has a dipolar structure such that no event is only physical or only mental. What is more, abstractions are already infused in all cosmic appearances of physical events: matter is never without some mentality. Physicalism or materialism is a mere abstraction from actual processes—which will be important for Whitehead's criticism of scientific materialism (as discussed in Sphere II). Furthermore, both dualities are related through the concept of "prehension." The relation between events is always one from the external past to the internal self-constitution. Neither can there be only a causally closed reality (cause-effect circularity), or only a measurable side to events, or two dualistically separated realities of mind and matter. Rather, as there can never be only one event (since it must become from others), there can be no distinction between subjects of experiences and objects of experiences that does not move into one another in the oscillation between these two dualities. This is the reason that Whitehead resisted Kant's claim of the inaccessibility of external reality to the mind and also the reversed his order of projection (Sphere V): not does the world only appear as a projection within the patterns of mind, but the mind always arises anew out of patterns of physical reality (as it is also inherently of such prehensive structures). Different from Heidegger's anthropocentric concentration of *Dasein* (the being that is "in the world" and in which Being arises) to consciousness, prehensive structures pervade Whitehead's universe regardless of consciousness—neither can we claim that consciousness should be reduced to only one mode, the human mode.

Furthermore, events are markedly different from things or substances. While things are presupposed to just exist, only their change being recognized as activity, events are constituted by the oscillation between concrescent becoming and transitional being and, hence, express a more fundamental activity that equally sustains persistence through time as well as change. From the perspective of the events of a table, for instance, it is as remarkable that it does not disappear, as it is that it does. The world, in Whitehead's process universe, exists in vast collections and patterns of events that create space-time always anew from the pulsating relations of those of events and evermore complex organisms they can manage to build (Exploration 2). Hence, a world that constitutes itself as becoming from such events is also markedly different from one that—in the classical view of Aristotle—was understood by the difference between substance and attribute. A substance is a thing insofar as it is essentially identical throughout time and in its essence, while change is a matter of the metamorphosis of more or less nonessential attributes. In such a world any individual thing is the only one that has access to itself; it is intrinsically self-existent. Contrarily, in a world of events nothing can be without the process of becoming of relations to other becoming actualities. In this world, nothing is self-identical, atomistic, isolated, and self-existent. It is not constituted through nothing but itself, but by everything, its whole world. This is, of course, of utmost importance when we seek the best categories to speak about God: should we choose (with classical metaphysics and theology) to imagine God in the image of a substance, as highest form of self-dependence, or should we understand God as highest form of relationality?

If reality is constituted by such webs of prehensive experiences, not only can we begin to understand why Whitehead uses the image of "drops of experience" to indicate these events, but we can also begin to fathom why he thought that such drops are constituted by, and are transmitting, *feelings* of their being in the world. Again, Whitehead does not restrict these moods of existence to humanity, like Heidegger. Even more, neither does he bind this feeling-existence to consciousness nor divorce it from consciousness. What this means is that whatever is experiencing and experienced is the procedure or outcome of valuations of potentials in light of the history of an event and naturally carries with it the valuations of these experiences in transmissions or creates new ones in the process of its self-constitution. Feelings can be conscious, they can be emotional (full of fear or hope, or love, or sorrow), but they always have a tone to themselves beyond the mere content or object they perceive or transmit. Such was the feelings of the car accident—fear and hope—and so were the events entering in it from its past—the tiredness of the morning, the sorrows of the last day, and so on. Whitehead speaks of every event, in some measure, as being constituted not only by the subject of experience (the becoming event) and the objects of experience (the past events, the potentials), but also a "subjective form," a *mode* of prehension and transmission.

Finally, events are self-creative processes. While this might not be so obvious with the example of the car accident, it is even implicitly present in its case. Since the possibilities and other elements of decision (of all involved participants) while the accident happens determine the outcome of the event, and not a predetermined cause-effect determinism, the mental reality of this complex event allows for alternatives that come to a "satisfaction" when all potential alternatives are exhausted—and not before this moment does the event become a fact of this accident or this close encounter. It creates itself from its decisions. We can, of course, think of more creative events as increasingly novelty, the unexpected, enters the picture: for instance, a surprising combination of words to the beauty of a poem. Although, like Heidegger, Alain Badiou has confined his understanding of events to rare historical novelties (like the French Revolution), it would be true to say in concordance with Badiou that an event happens in a situation (a world, a past), but cannot, when it happens be deducted from it. As an event is, in this sense, internal *and* external to its situation, every event, in Whitehead's sense, is self-creative; it is beyond its world. In rare cases, such as rare events of religious importance, we can definitely speak of a highly unprecedented irruption of novelty—such as is claimed by Christianity of the Christ event.

If Whitehead understands God in the image of the event (as analyzed here)—as he also does for human experiences and even persons—we must apply all of the developed aspects to God without forgetting that this is an image that imposes limitations on our thought, not on God. Hence, Whitehead never forgets that God is to be understood from experience first, and in this experience appears as the event in which all of the events of the world are related in oneness. This oneness will be addressed later, as well as the specific applications of the event terminology analyzed here (Sphere III). But one thing can be said already: the God event is neither abstracted from the whole world as mere transcendence, since it is the event in which the world exists; nor can God be excluded from appearing in the horizon of the world of events as unique event, as revelation, as manifestation (Exploration 16). As I will analyze later, this duality of the God event is essential to most of religious history and hence gives process theology an interesting transreligious instrument at hands to understand religious history as one of unity in diversity—as God is such an event-unity in diversity.

Exploration 2

ORGANISMS (SOCIETIES AND PERSONS)

IT IS A DIRECT implication of Whitehead's analysis of events that events must always be related to other events (Exploration 1). Most of the analysis of Whitehead's "philosophy of organism" in *Process and Reality* is committed to the understanding of this basic principle of processual relationality of all existence. Since no event can be alone, its prehensive relation with other events takes the form of a moment in a series and of a place in a landscape. That is, time and space are the expressions of the processual becoming of such nexuses of events in a temporal and a spatial sense. Counter to a classical view of space and time, for instance, in a Newtonian universe, which took them to be absolute entities themselves in which and through which things move, the event universe relativizes space and time insofar as they are the outcome of self-creative processes (of concrescence), being implications of its the factual outcome (transition), the fact of having become. This follows from the two polarities of events, namely, on the one hand, that of physical and mental poles, by which every event takes in the factual (temporal and special) past into its own internal becoming in contrasting them with its potentials of becoming, which are neither in space nor time, and, on the other hand, that of concrescence and transition, which indicates the shift from the internal becoming to that of an external reality. Every event becomes mentally (internally) a process of valuation of past facts and its cloud of potentials "outside" of the space-time continuum (but always related to it) in order to, finally, end up as a new quantum *of* space-time. This is the first insight in relation to the constitution of a universe of things: that things are located in space and time is really the outcome of processes that create the space-time continuum in the first place. Hence, as an implication, factual physical reality is not self-contained and it is not contained by space and time, but both are somehow the outcome of the workings of the two dualities of the creative processes that produce container and contained. Materialism is, therefore, an illusion, or at least a reduction of this becoming to only its physical side (Sphere II). Conversely, mental reality is productive of space-time and things, and, hence, "mind" is already interwoven with the production of the quantifiable universe, although the universe cannot exhibit mind without the participation of the "observer" in the observed. That this relates to the new physics of relativity theory (that there is no container of absolute space-time independent of what happens "in" it) and quantum physics (that the superposition of probabilities is rather a mental than a physical reality, at least in Bohr's Copenhagen interpretation) shall only be hinted at here.

Since events are connected through prehensive experiences, another implication is inevitable: experiences must have some content. Experiences are feelings of past experiences and feelings of potentials; they are decisions of *how* to perceive, of *how* to self-realize these experiences, and of *how* to transmit its own way to unify the world it finds in order to become another drop of experience of this world. So, this feeling is a vector of activity, giving it a direction, mediated through the insistence of the past in the present and the in-sistence of the self-creative event: it transmits a *content* to experience, which is the object of new experiences, through a process of valuations of its factual reality (any fact must be a definite fact, this or that, but never just "a" fact) and its inherent potentials open to further realization; and these facts transmit themselves as facts *of* valuations of their world of facts and potentials, that is, with their own *mode* (tone or mood) of becoming. Hence, the basic ingredients of this vector process of transition are, first, a world of facts and potentials that Whitehead calls "actual occasions" and "eternal objects" respectively; second, a perspective for which this is a world, that is, the potential landscape of the new actual entity in becoming, which Whitehead calls "initial aim" of an event; and, third, the modes of feeling by which the valuation in the facts are felt and evaluated and in self-creative decisions transmitted again, which Whitehead calls the "subjective forms" of becoming.

Experiences form *patterns* of the integration of a world of facts (actual entities), a cloud of potentials (eternal objects), of potential developments (aims), modes of feeling (subjective forms), and valuation processes (decisions), collected from (and though) the two poles, physical and mental, to become something, a definite event in the realization of all potentials reaching their exhaustion (satisfaction), their subjective integration (subjective aim), and their transition to other events (Sphere II). That is, events transcend themselves in a patterned form to become effective in other worlds of other events. In this function, Whitehead calls them "superjects." As a process of transmission of patterns, events not only form a nexus with others, but also transmit with their vector energy "information," that is, the pattern inherent in the content and mode of prehension. It is these patterns of eternal objects and subjective forms, inherent in the past actual facts, the real and pure potentials of their, and the new occasion's, process of decision, and transmitted with their superjective self-transcendence, that allow the created space-time to be coming from, and be harboring, structures of events, differentiations of transmitted traits, an interplay of order and novelty, the organization of a universe.

A universe is a structured intersection of nexuses of events and their worlds (from which they come and to which they contribute), exhibiting vast complex layers of such patterns of becoming and transmission. The connected universe is really a plethora of organisms perpetuating their characters, or changing them. And the more general orders of patterns we can call traits of societies and, regarding the universe as a whole, laws of nature. An organism is a combination of patterned transmission of events with more or less settled order, more or less creative change, or, in other words, a complex layered character of nested societies. A "society," in Whitehead's sense, is any spatial or/ and temporal nexus of events that shares some common characteristic pattern that all of its members uphold in the process of their reproduction of their individual traits (and despite their differences among themselves). This "common form of definiteness" or "defining characteristic" or "common element of form" or "substantial form" is what constitutes "enduring creatures" or "enduring objects" or "things."

And since all things, in Whitehead's process reconstruction, are societies of structurally related events, three things follow: first, the world does not consist of substances with a fixed self-identical form through time and representing an essence of which change is a mere modulation of dispensable qualities, but rather a collection of events in process of the self-creative constitution and transmission of patterns of feeling, which, if they are upheld, form characteristics or forms of transmission and perpetuation. Second, since information is not an abstract reality (except thought of as mere abstraction, as mere potential, as eternal object), but a pattern of feeling within, and between, processes of becoming that allows for differentiation, concreteness, and structural complexity, any concrete "entity" in the universe is an organism, that is, really a society of occasions, or a (more complex) society of societies of events. Third, insofar as societies perpetuate their characteristics throughout time, they look like substances, but they lack their untouchable essence, which is really only a perpetuated vector pattern of feelings having gone through perpetual processes of actual decisions. In direct reversal of Plato (and what many think defines Platonism), the forms in becoming are forms *of* becoming, not essences actualizing themselves in the shadow of matter, but potentials of actualizations exhibited by the characteristics of societies.

Insofar as such societies transmit their form throughout time (and thereby create time with such qualifications), Whitehead speaks of them as "persons." A person, hence, is, like a society, not anthropomorphically reduced to either humanity or consciousness. Rather, persons have become general descriptions of a universe in which human expressions are made possible by developments of the evolution of societies without being necessitated by them. Any personal society that does not just perpetuate itself regardless, but that admits novelty and change, Whitehead calls a "living person"—this can, of course, be an animal or a human, or maybe even another creature (only appearing in our dreams or assumed to be from another world). The more a person exhibits not only characteristic traits, but includes strong impulses of creativity, the more it is alive and the expression of what it means to live. In this sense, Whitehead finds the most intense realization of life in the most intense integration of order and novelty in an organism. He thinks of such an organism not only to harbors personal characteristics, but a "soul." Since with Aristotle Whitehead defines "soul" as a principle of being alive and since life means novelty, instead of the perpetuation of essential characteristic, a living soul is the most extravagant expression of the transmission of intensities of feeling *and* a creativity that cannot be reduced to structural integrity, but is the most excellent manifestation of originality.

Here, we can sense one of the most intriguing paradoxes in Whitehead's organic thought. Life, for Whitehead, is not itself a society. Since originality defines life, the more a personal society lives, the more it becomes asocial, a-structural, a-characteristic. Yet, no living originality can do without a social structure that perpetuates the societies only in which, on which, for which a living occasion or nexus can be alive. This means the more a person is alive, the more they are prone to destroy the very basis of their existence, namely, the characteristic of a society that not only harbors and shelters its living occasions, but is disintegrated by the weight of their creative originality. The paradoxical center of a living person, then, is not their character, but their "entirely living nexus" that perpetually attacks the character of stability, but could not exist without it. Hence, the greatest feat of organic life, for Whitehead, is the integration of harmony and intensity in form of a highest-level balance between the organicity (structural integrity) of a character of a living society *and* the freedom of unbound originality, perpetual novelty, and spontaneous difference. This, in fact, is impossible, since absolute life (in the defines meaning) and death (of the supporting organism) would coincide. Instead, becoming (and staying) alive and becoming ever more alive is a process of the ever-new evaluation of such a balance that can never reach its own balance, because then it would have become a character instead of remaining spontaneous. Hence, imbalance is the motor of an unending process of ever-new integrations of this harmony of intensities.

There are two ways in which Whitehead addresses this conundrum of living persons. Process theologians often retraced the first one; the second one is mostly uncharted. The first way orients itself more toward structural integrity. The higher the integration, the more such a living personal society is hierarchically structured (with complexly nested societies of societies building its organism). In this sense, Whitehead understands plants to exhibiting less centralization (unlike animals if they developed a nervous system) and, hence, to (ironically) display a less hierarchical, more "democratic" organization. Yet, conversely, their novelty cannot be canalized to express higher-grade freedom of self-integrated persons. Animal organization, however, exhibit a hieratical organization of self-integration, which allows them to loosen the limitations of, and to expand their degrees, of (physical and mental) movement. In humans, then, a leading personal society of highly conscious events (a soul) is integrated in, but differentiated from, the bodily organism to form the transmission of the ever-new balance of structural integrity and originality.

The alternative model that I have favored in my own work is more oriented toward the asocial side of originality.

Since, in any case, a soul cannot be a substance, but indicates the nexic flow of a living person, Whitehead expresses the view that what actually makes up the person as such is neither organization (hierarchy) nor novelty (chaos) per se, but the very *space* that constitutes the togetherness of events as such, in the concrete life history of a certain organism. On this view, a person is not a (separate) soul, but also not a (separate) body of the collected experiences thought space and time, but the contiguity of the most basic interrelationship of its events. In other words, a person is a drop of the expansive medium of existence *itself* on the most basic level (in Whitehead's analysis), namely, of the mutual immanence of (all) events. In *Adventures of Ideas*, Whitehead follows Plato's analysis of *khora*, of *hypodoche*, of the "place" of existence, of the "receptacle" of existence, of the foster mother of becoming, to make this suggestion (Exploration 3).

Many traces could be drawn out from this analysis of societies and persons in Whitehead. I will only highlight three of them. First, Whitehead demonstrates a thoroughly ecological thinking, neither anthropocentrically reductive nor dualistic in dividing reality in independent spheres of mind and matter. Rather all is interwoven in the production of a world of societies and persons, geared toward evermore intense form of life and originality, but in a perpetual process of harmonious integration and reintegration. Society and person are not human phenomena; rather human organization—biologically as well as sociologically—is a mere expression of the deep nature of things. Second, mind and body condition one another not as levels, but as ingredients of organization. Order is a characteristic of the mental structuring of physical creatures, and physical creatures are creative bearers of mentality. Creativity and life are matters of course of organizations of organisms that allow for the differentiation of a mentality that can extract itself from its organic environment in the form of creative alternatives to its physical past, without losing its connections with physicality, as the physical universe is their own self-realization for the perpetuation of life. Third, as societies are implicit evolutionary necessities of the connectivity of a universe of events as processes of the feeling of interrelations, so are persons evolutionary necessities of social organization that spans space-time with patterns of order and potentials of novelty. Not that any specific organization of societies and persons would be more than a potential of the processual relationality of events—humanity is not a necessity, but a contingency of the necessity of this processual structure— but we can say that, without any particular direction or restriction, the development of ever-higher forms of the organizational (organic) integration of societies to living persons is inevitable if creativity should come forth as a driving force. The highest forms of integration, hence, must be personal streams of life with entirely living nexuses at their core, being (at the same time) able to harmoniously relate to their body, society, and universe in such a way that neither order destroys its novelty nor novelty gets lost in the transmission of its characteristics.

Religious connotations abound. If God relates to such a universe of societies and persons, God must never be less than their highest expression in releasing modes of harmonization and intensification for the self-creative evolution of ever more living societies. If God is to be understood in the image of an event, God cannot be just one event among others, but must embrace the whole plethora of societies and persons. Indeed, not only must God relate to the universe as God's body, in some sense, being its "soul"—the *atman*, the world-soul of Plotinus and of the *Bhagavat Gita*, is not far away—rather, God must be that entirely living nexus in which all possible worlds have their place as potentials for actualization in the world or the worlds (in an infinite plural), but also harbor all societies and persons in Godself as a unity that only such an event can exhibit. Indeed, in his late article "Immortality" (1941), Whitehead will characterize God as personality of all personalities. Yet, since God is not a society—remember, an entirely living nexus, harboring life to the utmost, is not a society—God is rather what the biblical tradition has called Spirit and the Hindu tradition Brahman. And as any person, on my reading of the khoric nature of personhood, is not a soul substance, so is God not a soul substance, but in some sense *khora* itself as the foster mother of becoming: *atman* is *brahman*. But as God event, again, as God unity in diversity, God is not identical to this cosmic space either, but rather signifies its *pneuma*, its spirit person. This brings us to the question of the nature of the universe as a whole, which will be the theme of the next exploration (Exploration 3).

Exploration 3

THE MULTIVERSE

ALTHOUGH IT MIGHT BE tempting to use the conceptual components making up Whitehead's understanding of the universe in organismic terms to think of the whole universe as one organism—maybe even with God as its immanent world soul (and some process thinkers, like Charles Hartshorne, have come close to this image), this would be premature without taking into account Whitehead's complex rendering of the most basic features conceptualizing the universe cosmologically and theologically. In the first place, the God event cannot be an organism in the sense of mutually constructing and deconstructing, becoming and perishing layers of societies, even if it has an entirely living nexus as its core (a "soul," as it were) since it releases and embraces all of them without being identical to any of them. God as event exhibits a unity that is equally more one than any society and more differentiated because of its all-embracing expansiveness. Since nothing is "outside" of

God, we can speak of this God event to concur with forms of panentheism (which will be explored further in Exploration 11). Yet, as this unity of the God event is also incomparable with any world event, it is rather indicating the difference between God and the world *itself* than being just different from any event or their difference from another. At the same time, we could say that God is more differentiated than any world at any stage of its process since God embraces and release all possible worlds for realization and cannot in any way deny their actualizations, that is, must bear them in all their diversity.

The universe, then, can also not be captured under the image of an organism since it is unified only by the most profound impossibility of any absolute isolation between any given events, nexuses, societies, or worlds. However, it is, on this basis, only existing as an always self-differentiating process developing into more and more different and more complex organisms, none of them being able to comprise the whole of this differentiation or the space-time continuum all of them might create together as their virtual home—a home in permanent change through the ongoing process of becoming. This is the reason that Whitehead never equated God with the world and, hence, avoided finding any "unity" of the organisms proliferating into divergent multiplicities that would undermine this movement of differentiation—forcefully cutting diversions off or stopping the process as such. It is for this reason that Whitehead, when he tries to conceptualize the unity of the universe, speaks only in these terms of it: first, the universe is a multiplicity that cannot be subsumed under any unity that would not again be a multiplicity. The opposite of this view is what Whitehead really tried to avoid at all costs: namely, a holistic nesting of levels of unity, comprised by a super-unity, because in such a universe the process would have to come to a halt. Second, the universe is united *as* a process; process is the equivalent of the universe as one; that is, the very movement of the processual relationality of events, nexuses, and societies is ultimate. This is the reason that Whitehead called these three "things"—events (actual entities), nexuses, and societies—the ultimate expression of actual reality, insurmountable by, and irreducible to, anything else more concrete. Conversely, anything else would be only a conceptual abstraction from their concreteness of existence. Herein also lies the reason that God (as event, nexus, or society, respectively) is not an abstraction, even if God is a much more different unity (from either of them). Third, the unity of the universe is—as has been hinted at already (Exploration 2)—that of a mutuality of relationality that Whitehead captures with the term *hypodoche* (and *khora*), which he takes from the Dialogue *Timaeus* wherewith Plato seeks to name the "place," the "wherein," of becoming, differentiated from the ideas, actualities, and the demiurge. Fourth, the universe is united by the exhibition of the very activity without which nothing would happen. Whitehead calls this reality "creativity"—in some sense the ultimate reality of a becoming universe. Yet, even creativity is only "one" in abstraction *from* the actualities, but *in* which is the indication of their self-creativity and transition. That is, creativity is the immanent reality of becoming itself and beyond that only an abstraction.

At the beginning of *Process and Realty*, were Whitehead discusses the categories of his undertaking of a cosmology, he finds a truly magical formula to describe his conceptual intuition of the unity of the universe *as* relational process. What he calls the "category of the ultimate" captures the essence of the one creative process thus: *the many become one and are increased by one.* Three elements comprise this ultimate category as relational process: the *many* actualities (the disjunctive past of new becoming, the potential actual world of future events), the *one* new actuality (uniting the past actualities in some way and with some tone mediated by the cloud of potentials and unrealized possibilities), and *creativity*, the measure of novelty (either of new events to come into existence, even if they are just repeating their past character, but even more so if the new realization can actualize new possibilities hitherto not found in the past actual world of an event). The grammar of this process, as addressed in this twofold formula, is important here: not only is a creative process one of the unification of the many, but with equal force is a process in which every unification differentiates the continuum of a world of which it becomes part insofar as it adds it own becoming to it. In the form of this dual oscillation we can now see why no unity can ever unite the *all* of multiplicity, namely, because any unity must become part of the multiplicity, a new multiplicity it helped to cerate by uniting its world and releasing itself into a new world enriched by itself.

Coming back to the question, what is the universe if it is not an organism, a society, an event, or the like? I will answer: it is a complex, layered, nested environment of organisms, nexuses, and events, but is neither of them, except in a very special, extremely universal sense. Think of it from the perspective of any organism within an environment. Any organism can only exist if its environment tolerates it, that is, if the environment exhibits the characteristics of a society that is favorable to a nested society with its more specific rules—much like a fish that cannot survive on land, because the specific biological characteristics of its respiratory system are not provided for by the characteristics of the physics and chemistry of air. On a more general level, biological organisms, with their physical, chemical, and biological characteristics, can only exist in an environment that allows for elementary particles to have bonded and allowed for the emergence of chemical reactions. So, no such organism can survive in the early stage of the universe when these processes have not yet taken place.

In the most general sense, Whitehead abstracts the nesting environments as societies with more general characteristic allowing or forfeiting the specific rules of more special societies. Biological organisms need environments of physical and chemical bonding processes. A society of electromagnetic fields will be a specific society of fields in space-time. Three-dimensional space-time will be a specific society within a society that exhibits geometrical relations (spaces can have more or less than three dimensions, and maybe they are physically even in this universe of that nature). The geometrical society will be just one of the possible societies of extension, which may be beyond any patterns of dimensionality.

The most general society thinkable would be the one that encompasses with necessity *any* possible other society. It would approximate to a characterization of the utmost boundary of what any world whatsoever would define. There are only two alternatives left for Whitehead: mere possibility and mere extension. However, the problem is that both options would have abstracted from any actual world, as an actual world would need to exhibit creativity, that is, activity of becoming. Hence, whatever the choice between the two, they do not amount to the constitution of "worlds," but will always indicate only abstractions from any world. Furthermore, both possibility and extension cannot be understood as unity, but only as utmost boundary concept of multiplicity, that is, they do not exhibit any characteristic that would define a society. For these reasons, the realms of possibility and of extension are not societies, but in themselves only chaos. In other words, they only amount to modes of what I call the chaotic nexus.

Nevertheless, Whitehead ingeniously recognizes that this chaotic nexus, being the sheer definition of the nexus (over against any society with characteristics), as long as it must be the real basis of any world (which always is an actual world), is not what we—in out substantialist mode of thinking—might expect it to be, namely, featureless chaos. Rather, it exhibits *one* feature defining *any* nexus at all, and that is connectivity—that chaos is a connected multiplicity (at least exhibiting the impossibility of total unconnectedness)! In *Adventures of Ideas, any* nexus, *the* ultimate nexus, is defined only by the *mutual immanence* of its multiplicity of events, nothing more. But, thereby, any world is already some form, process, or pattern of interconnectedness. This is Whitehead's restatement of Plato's *khora*: as the ultimate matrix of existence, the foster mother of becoming, the ultimate medium of intercommunication.

This mutual immanence—like all of Whitehead's concepts—exhibits the duality of process and relationality. As it must be a prehensive connection, it is one of events in process, not things or substances. Its multiplicity is, therefore, creative activity and expansive continuity. Its two sides are "creativity," by which the rhythm of concrescence and transition moves towards the perpetual novel constitution of the universe its events span, *and* "extensive continuum," by which this universe never loses its connectivity throughout the spatiotemporal expansiveness of its existence.

One of the fascinating consequences of this understanding of the constitution of any universe is that Whitehead can incorporate the concept of the multiverse (although he does not use this word). There are of course today many different variations to understand this term: from the quantum physical interpretation of a splitting universe in every moment of the breakdown of the wave function of Hugh Everett to the bubble bath universe of Leonard Susskind, from the eternal inflation of Alexander Vilenkin to the actuality of all possible worlds of David Lewis, and many more. Not that Whitehead's cosmology would be indifferent to the plurality of these conceptualizations, but instead of discussing the respective restraints of Whitehead's multiverse in relation to these current theories, I will name some of its ingenuous features. First of all, it appears in a theory of "cosmic epochs." This conceptualization is based on the presuppositions hitherto discerned: that no characteristics besides mutual immanence define the chaotic nexus on which all universes must be based; that infinite possibilities allow for infinite many worlds, each bound together by the extensive continuum within which any of its characteristics develop or settle; and that the characteristics that determine a specific universe as a society are introduced by the persistent repetition of creative decisions of events eventually informing this universal nexus as a society. Hence, even natural laws are such characteristics of societies, which cannot be just presupposed as a fixed set, as they are in themselves only possibilities in compatible combination for actualization, decided only by the cosmic society that upholds them. This means these characteristics could drift out of there general applicability when the events in such a society move to other creative conditions—and those, in turn, would become universally accepted. The "unity" of such a metastable universe is what Whitehead calls a cosmic epoch. Any universe could move to other conditions or move through a chaotic loss of its characteristics or pulsate between phases of chaos and (always different) order or shift between orders or develop into unrealized potential orders.

Despite the potential implication that this landscape can only be one single line of universes (a single series of cosmic epochs)—as some process thinkers have defended—I would, instead, refer to the strangeness of potential conditions of universes in Whitehead's oeuvre in favor of a more complex multiplicity of worlds (and world series). Here are three such strange conditions: first, since God is intimately involved with the arrangement of possibilities through divine valuation of all possibilities, not all worlds are equally desirable, and hence, some may never be realized. The phrase "all possible worlds," in Whitehead's understanding, means worlds that have potentials for intensity and harmony, not possibilities that lack these criteria of valuation. They are based on the goodness of God (Exploration 12). Second, "time" is not a defined constant. This means that Whitehead can imagine a world in which the event structure is such that the perpetual perishing of events is suspended. In such a world, novelty would not mean loss. Here, Whitehead comes close to diverse religious imaginations of redeemed worlds. Third, the relation between cosmic epochs cannot be defined by any notion of space and time related to, and defined by, *our* universe. Hence, whether there are parallel worlds or we can imagine a diversifying tree of universes or just one line of universes is undecided by their specific characteristics (like space and time) with which we might try to restrict our imagination of their diversity.

Whitehead's understanding of the involvement of God in the universe is intriguing (Sphere III), but differs from a mere theory of "God's mind," as developed, for instance, by the Canadian philosopher John Leslie (and the theologian Keith Ward, although Ward does not acknowledge the fast extent to which he is dependent on Whitehead). While similar restrictions apply to the mind of God and while

Whitehead's God can be understood in some sense as such a mind of the universe, for Whitehead, as the most differing characteristic, the multiverse does not exist just *in* the mind of God. Rather, the multiverse is an expression of the infinity of divine potentials for actualization through the creativity of the world, but its actuality, and God's reception of its actuality, is not just a product of divine mentality (Exploration 12). Hence, the insistence of Whitehead that the multiverse consist of the mutual immanence of events, and that all events exhibit the dipolarity of mentality and physicality, subjectivity and objectivity, concrescence and transition. Hence, also Whitehead's insistence that God is not just mind (or the universal mind) or the world soul, but an *event*—also with a dipolarity of mentality and physicality. Hence, finally, Whitehead's insistence that God and creativity are not identical, but that creativity is shared between the God event and all world events and, therefore, that God is not a metaphysical principle (like creativity), but a unique concrete event (without being one among others, as was discussed earlier).

In any case, the search for the conditions of the universe have led us to the same conclusion we gained before regarding events, nexuses, and societies: namely, that the "unity" of the universe can itself not be captured with any fixed character or as integrated into one monumental thing. Rather, like the multiplicities of *khora*, creativity, possibilities, actualities, the multiverse can only exist as a multiplicity of processual relationality. The more we search out these functions, we will also realized how Whitehead's introduction of God furthers, not hinders or upsets, these insights: that God offers potentials and values for the process to reach ever new heights of intensity and harmony; that God prehends all events, nexuses, societies, and universes in God's memory; that God instigates the best creativity in all creatures; that divine unity of the process is itself processual and *for* a processual multiplicity of realizations—without beginning, unending.

SPHERE II

SCIENCE, PHILOSOPHY, AND RELIGION

THE MOST PROFOUND DECISIONS in the process under-standing of reality in connection with divinity—as developed in Sphere I—have not arisen in a hermetic space, but reflect the horizon in which this new view could be born, namely, as an answer to the corrosion of the scientific, philosophical, and religious integrities formed in the preceding centuries. The "turn of the century"—to the twentieth century—was not only one of major developments in the study of the sciences, but also one of new philosophical outlooks and new approaches to the study of religion. Although all of these fields of investigation were based on a long history, the face they now presented, their very constitution as fields or methods, was the consequence of a profound fragmentation of the integrated worldview that preceded them. In other words, their new appearance reflected the disintegration of the inherited models of social discourse and political will. The totalitarian ideologies of the twentieth century were an investment in a lost cause: in a project to reinvigorate these long faded integrities (even in the form of bizarre reinstatements of patriarchy, colonialism, nationalism, racism, and capitalism)—as was the perpetuated defense of Enlightenment reason in its use as an integrating instrument over against the perceived forces of disintegration, which came to be called the postmodern condition, the loss of superstructures, super-narratives, naïve holisms, naïve expectations of human progress, and so on.

The rivalry between science, philosophy, and religion at this "turn" is one of the most visible signs of the intellectual havoc of the war between forces of deconstruction and forces of reintegration—both weaponized with sharp verbal instruments of mutual dismissal, on occasion, instigating or justifying social, political, and ideological violence. One has only to remember the impact and involvement that the sciences, ideologies, and religious justifications had in and around the two world wars on the war machines, the industrial rationality of the Shoah, or the atom bomb (and its derivatives). Without getting into a futile game of cause and effect, we can acknowledge the implications of the mutual denigrations between science and philosophy (the death of philosophy), science and religion (the death of religion), as well as philosophy and (the study of) religion by revisiting the splits that their respective ideological engagement in reconstruction and disintegration forced on their fields. Within science, we witness the cleavage between old Newtonian and new Einsteinian science, between relativity theory and quantum physics, between modern and postmodern science, but also reintegration efforts through (physicalist) reductionism or evolutionism. Within philosophy, we recognize the splintering between continental and analytic philosophy, modern and postmodern philosophy, positivism and existentialism, but also reintegration efforts through materialist reductionism and holistic integral philosophies. And within the study of religion, we recognize the fragmentation between the apologetic and the critical study of religion, between theology and religious studies (*Religionswissenschaft*), between western and eastern (studies of) religion, between the Abrahamic siblings, between spirituality and religiosity, intellectual access and piety, dogmatic orthodoxies and experiential mysticisms, militant conservatism and atheism, but also reintegration efforts through reductionism of religious realities to sociology or neuroscience, on the one hand, and universally tolerant movements of religious pluralism and comparative as well as cross-cultural studies and interspiritual practices, on the other.

It is in the broad context of these social, political, and intellectual forces that Whitehead's sensitivities toward process and relationality, the cosmos as a community of becoming, and the epistemological as well as ontological ideal of unity in diversity have taken shape in his own philosophy as well as the emergent tradition of process theology, wandering through this landscape and coping with the still forceful impacts of this "turn," now having become a new turn of a century. It will be important to realize that Whitehead, as a basic rule, chose to refuse any kind of reductionism as a reaction to, and solution for, this situation. Yet, it will be equally important to keep in mind that he never did embrace any naïve holism or integralism as well. Furthermore, while Whitehead was generally always operating under the defense of novelty over against (a mere repetition of) tradition—for instance, by using Einsteinian and quantum physics against classical reductionisms—he deviated from any form of hyper-modernism or postmodernism when they lost track of either the poetic (over the merely mechanical) nature of reality (forgetting the inherent processuality of becoming) or seemed to indulge in mere fragmentation of pluralities (thereby forgetting the inherent relationality of becoming). Finally, Whitehead, in general, accepted the inherent worth of all of these areas of study—science, philosophy, and religion—as immanent to, and based on, universal patterns of experience, being differentiated in their mode of realizing reality, but also being connected by a general scheme of experience in a world of divine-mundane intercourse through mutual processuality and relationality. With this context, the characteristic forces of the "turn," as well as of the general reaction of Whitehead to this situation in mind, we can now, in more detail, rehearse the inner workings of the Whiteheadian counter-propositions.

Whitehead's project, to which process theology (in the sense already developed) knows itself to be indebted, we can say, pursues a twofold aim. On the one hand, the Whiteheadian project wants to discover means for the transformation of (any and all possible) categories and strategies into peaceful contrasts, whether it be regarding thought or moral action. On the other hand, the Whiteheadian project wants to also develop instruments for such a transformation, which, for this reason, would need to be not only instruments for a critical analysis, but also for an entirely new synthesis of the fragmented, but inescapably connected realms of science, philosophy, and religion. Both sides of this project come to reveal their integrity when we ask how Whitehead understands them to relate: in Whitehead's final analysis, science and religion form the sister forces that will determine the emergence of a civilization of the future *if* it should ever be born at all. And philosophy, in this triangulation, is for Whitehead the medium of the mutual mediation of science and religion.

Most importantly, then, Whitehead's philosophical coinhabitation of all three spheres, especially in view of their social relevance, is meant to focus on the critique of those abstractions that have managed to posit these spheres of influence vis-à-vis as if they were (and must be) in antagonistic competition and a constant battle. It is precisely in the presupposed mutual isolation of these three spheres (and the further splits within themselves) that Whitehead detects the wasted land it left behind, filled with the destructive forces that deformed the historical development of the Occident to its imperialistic and colonialist generalization over humanity as a whole throughout the period of the recent centuries.

For this historical effect, however, Whitehead does not only cite political and social forces, but also the schemes of thought that have made them possible and, like a sedimentary deposit, have laid their destructive capacities aground as if they were reality itself. Since Whitehead is convinced that no human development was ever devoid of accompanying schemes of thought and worldviews, he tries to recover their destructive and constructive potentials alike by exposing their common methodological assumption: that any analysis must want to discover the most simple of their basic elements since they, like mental atoms, have become invisible in their effect throughout all of the layers of their combination and recombination. It is, however, the irony of these simplifications that their categorical reductions also assume reality to consist of to self-identical building blocks. The methodological and epistemological simplifications, thereby, not only help to erect a world scheme consisting of atoms or self-identical, independent conglomerates of stable, hermetical entities in a void. Rather, any programmatic striving for knowledge and understanding of this kind has managed to effectively limit the search to the discovery of only such atomistic, substance-like, simple realities. The lens of inspection only finds what it seeks. It does, however, not find what it finds because such a world actually exists; rather what it finds is the only reality that can be found by those means.

In Whitehead's understanding, therefore, it is the task of philosophy to critique such (atomistic, fragmented, reductionist, simplified) foundations as fictional constructs of certain modes of abstract thinking, and the weight given to them by attaching reality to them. It is in this context that we might begin to understand why (and even in what form) Whitehead begins to develop his own alternative metaphysical categories: not by banning such abstractions as if they have not had real effects on history, but by unmasking them *as* abstractions in their limitations so as to make them *as such* (*as* abstractions) available for constructive alternatives. To say it again: Whitehead does not despise abstractions (concepts, propositions, generalizations, and the like) as such, but *only insofar* as they are used so as to magically become basic to an analysis of reality, because then they are mistaken to be the more profound reality before, and for, any analysis. Conversely, by discovering and acknowledging this plethora of abstractions as what it is, not reality but abstraction from it, abstractions can take on an entirely different function for an entirely different worldview. Instead of being one of simplification, reductionism, fragmentation, Whitehead proposes a worldview in which vibrating patterns of movements of becoming explain such abstractions as moments of their inherent process of self-constitution and communication. And at the same time, Whitehead illuminates them in such a way that they can now point toward their own dangerousness *if* (and as long as) they are confounded with reality. Now, in the search for reality, they cannot escape anymore into, or hide under, the sedimentations, doing their invisible work of substituting reality, and instigating perpetual warfare. Now, abstractions can join in the assembly of becoming with a new lens in mind, which will shed an entirely different light on phenomena.

One of the ways Whitehead summarized the effects of these old schemes of thought was that of a philosophy that in one or another way reaches back to the beginning of Greek thought and became to an early victory in the thought of Plato and Aristotle, which began to influence virtually every occidental philosophy of later times: "substantialism." It conveys the idea that reality consists of self-sustaining, self-identical, and self-asserting blocks or entities of independent (ir-relational) essences (without processuality), which over their career of existence (in time) never change, except in their accidental features. Contrary to the substantialist triggers that have become effective in the waves of scientific revolutions since the Renaissance and that, with their inherent dualism of mind/spirit and matter, have contributed to the bifurcation of reality into material space-time (a timeless space filled with material entities) and subjective mentality of human reality (a timeless space filled with mental entities), Whitehead counters with the dethronement of their claims to absoluteness—absolute atoms, absolute space, absolute time. Surprisingly, his arguments were not confined to philosophical alternatives, but invoked and engaged the evidences of the new physics of the dawning 20th century. Isn't it with the strange relational complexities in relativistic and quantum mechanical dimensions that this new physics itself discovered a world of mutual relations? And doesn't this world, in its own turn, only in a very vague and abstract sense, give any (if at all) evidence to the categorical oppositions used to analyze them? In fact, the atomistic, substantialist reductionism that had fostered the discoveries of this new physics, did so not because they obeyed these categories, but because the categories failed to explain the phenomena.

And this is what Whitehead gleaned from the new physics for the new philosophical paradigm of reality: no (actual) entity is only where it is. It is rather a manifold of relations in this or any unique event that entangles space and time and the characteristic of its inheritance into an interwoven universe. Every actual entity is a happening, a process of such unifications and diversifications, and the cosmos amounts to a complex historical network of such congregations of happenings, of the inherent and changing patterns and their differentiation in communities of mutual amplification and diminution. This world is like a musical score in which the notes, at the same time, function as the musicians of their sounding, of these or those respective harmonies or disharmonies, of these or those respective intensities of their sound. Continuity, in this world, has a becoming. However, that which becomes is not inherently continuous (hermetically self-identical throughout time), but always already constituted, influenced, continued, or discontinued by others as it influences, constitute, continues, or discontinues others. In this world, they are not substances of self-identical, independent, self-sufficient, and unchanging endurance that lend a philosophical grid for reality (anymore), but events, actualities, occasions of becoming that grant access to deeper levels of reality as they genuinely exhibit the characteristics of processuality and relationality.

In his critique of substantialist thought, Whitehead, for the same reasons, sought to undermine the separation of reality as it appeared in the philosophical sects of idealistic, rationalistic, and empiricist provenience, which dominated the modern and Enlightenment epoch (after the breakdown of the medieval integralism). What is more, he also attached importance to the avoidance of the reductionist implications of both monistic and pluralistic models of reality that each in their own way tried (and still try) to escape the named dualisms, but were—in his analysis—still perpetuating the same substantialist presuppositions on a deeper level. Not dissimilar to the endeavor of Immanuel Kant to hold (or bring again) together these great streams of the philosophy of modernity, Whitehead ventured into developing a metaphysics of experience that unites the efforts of both rationalist and empiricist methodology as well as monist and pluralist outlook, each persisting in even stronger opposition to one another after the failure of the experiment of Kantian integralism. Whitehead saw the Kantian project fall short insofar as it actually could not unite, but had contributed to the dualistic separation of the empirical and the rational, unity and plurality, because the mutual delimitation of rational knowledge (insofar as it relates to experiences) and knowability of the world (through sensations) was based on their incompatibility and isolation. Contrary to the dualistic aporia of the unknowability of the external world beyond the subject of experience und the isolation of the subject from the reality experienced, Whitehead posits the new paradigm of the emergence of subjects of knowledge *from* their experiences (which are also their objects of experience).

We can again retrace his analysis by observing the categories of relation and process in play: Whatever exists (not only occurrences of human cognition) is in itself (against Kant's *ignotum x*) a process of experience, a process of growing together of a subject from its experiences. This is what Whitehead calls "concrescence"—a genial choice of terms since it indicates the concrete as in its essence always to be a process of becoming concrete, a growing together to the concreteness of the concrete reality that an actual reality is when it has become. The objects of the world, which are the actual world of such a process of concrescence, are always involved in this process by becoming the subjective world of the becoming event, the subject of their experience and of the experience of this as its world. That is, in this process the subject constitutes *itself* from and in experiences.

Here are a few terms with which Whitehead tries to conceptualize this relational process: the revolutionary concept of experience, as self-production of subjects from experiences of other subjects of experience that have become objects of its own becoming subject, Whitehead calls "prehension." It is an abbreviation of the term "apprehension" that was philosophically used to understand objects of experience in the unity of consciousness; yet, Whitehead wanted to express the universal cosmological use of such a process before and beyond, but not excluding, consciousness (thereby avoiding anthropocentrism in his understanding of experience). However, this is not only a process of collection and integration, but, even more, always in some way a creative process. It is through prehensions, then, that a becoming subject collects itself in a creative process in a certain way or mode, which Whitehead calls the "subjective form" of experiences or the tone of feeling, as it were, together into a new perspective on its world. And it does so sensitively to the past and creatively into a new future in light of the potentials inherent in the experiences and creative reflections on them. These potentials for becoming, whether from the past or as not yet realized possibilities, are what Whitehead, in a difficult term, calls "eternal objects." Since what will become in this process is a new unity of experience, it must in some sense be understood to have an internal projection of its own unification. Whitehead calls this the "subjective aim" of an event. When this unification process is exhausted, all of its potentials are either realized or excluded, and experiential unity is reached, Whitehead speaks of the "satisfaction" of an event. Now, it has not only become, it "is," but it has also become itself a new object for new happenings of such prehensive processes. Now, an event has transcended itself beyond its subjectivity and "acts" as "superject."

The technical description and analysis of these elements of processes in Whitehead's philosophy is elaborate and beyond the capacity of this introduction. What is important to remember, however, is that every existent being *actually* exists, both as subject, self-actualizing its own existence (realizing itself for itself), and as object, effectuating other existents (realizing what it is itself for others). It presents itself (to itself and others) as a process of experience of the world itself, as the way the world exists in these events (in present subjects) and consisting of them (as objects, as and insofar it is its past). It is the world, then, that unites itself, as it were, in every new event in unique ways (seeing itself from this particular perspective on itself). In this variably creative process of unification, each happening owns in itself a certain subjective quality of inwardness (immanence, immediacy) that will not even completely disappear in the perceived (prehended) objects of experience, because every process presents itself effectively (realizing itself in others) beyond its own processual existence as unique unity of *its* experiences. Every event is a relational process in which it feels other events and feels their feelings or tone of existence—something Martin Heidegger had called *Stimmung*, the mood of existence.

The element that fuses past and future, inheritance and novelty, actuality and potentiality, subject and object in Whitehead's non-substantialist scheme finally also reveals why every actual reality is the integration of fact and value and, hence, can neither be reduced to either a merely material or merely spiritual universe, or fall apart into two (Cartesian) parallel universes of such kinds. It is that element that makes the process of actualization actual, namely: that it is a process of *decision*. In Whitehead's metaphysical analysis of experience as a universal category of existence, every occurrence or happening is the unification of relations to *its* world: through its world, its facts and potentials for experience are presented; but the concrescent event is not necessarily bound by them. Instead of following mere reception (as in a mere cause-effect correlation), every event undergoes some kind of *creative process* with respect to the mode of its unification of its world relations. The creative freedom in such a process is correlative to its more or less complex potentials entertained or released by its world and by a cloud of unrealized, but realistic (that is, realizable) possibilities. This complex space of potentials for actualization again is modulated through a decision *how* and to what extend to be actualized in one or another way. Through this process of integrative and creative decision, the disjunctive many conjugate; and their creative unity again becomes part of a new relational manifold enriched by this process. But since this whole transformation is a process of *valuation*, it produces facts from values.

This move is meant to counter the "bifurcation of nature," that is, the splitting of the ecological network of relations of the world into the atomistic, substantialist conceptions entertained by scientific materialism. Whitehead's critique of science is not one of the empirical method, but of the philosophical content that the correlated theoretical approach to its method came to imply. Its materialism became a presupposition because of the accepted foundation of a dualism between mind and matter. It provoked a split of fact from value with the sphere of value now to only indicate an illusory remainder of a shadow realm of spirit/mind. This reductionist partition, again, was now used to justify a research program that seeks not only atomistic substances, but also (only) the atomistic truths of this material world. Conversely, it also triggered resistance against this reductionism ending up in on the other side of the split—spiritual flights into "other worlds"—without remedying the hiatus itself.

Here, Whitehead's non-reductionist, non-dualist, and non-substantialist approach, articulating a new metaphysical configuration of the processional and relational world, is important. On this proposition, every happening of and in the world is a relational interaction and processional oscillation between objective and subjective poles, facts and creative decisions, actuality and potentiality, effect and purpose, necessity and freedom, past and future, continuity and discontinuity, unity and multiplicity, permanent and impermanent elements. Hence, both (isolated) mind/spirit and matter are only constructive (constructed) abstractions of mental processes of simplification of our mind, as are the host of conceptual pairs just mentioned, and the metaphysical conceptions (or their denial) based on them. In order to signify these oscillating movements of relations of the cosmos, Whitehead uses the notion of *creativity*. It is that ontological plurisingularity that is only real in its actualizations (events) and beyond their concreteness (concrescence) is also only an abstraction. In its most universal application, creativity now also allows for the unification of the boundary concepts of God and the world by, at the same time, differentiating them. Hence, in Whitehead's ontology, the "Being of beings" is neither identified with God or the world nor is it, beyond their actualization, more than an abstraction *from* their reality.

This Whiteheadian unity in oscillation has now also important implications for the understanding of religion. Because of the relational and creative conception of the world process, Whitehead's critique of religion does not emanate from the dying abstractions produced by diverse religious orthodoxies or the disintegrations of religious concepts and realities through secular philosophical designs. Nor is his critique interested in the reduction of religion (and religions) to evolutionary realities, so prevailing a notion in 19th century criticisms of religion, be they of biological, psychological, social, or economic provenience—inevitably connected with the names of Charles Darwin, Sigmund Freud, Emile Durkheim, and Karl Marx. Since Whitehead takes seriously experiences of any kind, complexity, or level, he admits the *phenomenon* of religion and religious experience as genuine and irreducible, contrary to the ill-directed search for atomistic simplicities. Religious, mystical, and spiritual experiences are constructive perceptions of deeply intuited reality. Hence, Whitehead is interested in *how* reality reveals itself in those religious experiences (and how, then, religions reflect reality). Since they are expressions of relational and processional nature like any other experiences, such an analysis can now also reveal a connectedness with the ways experiences unfold themselves in scientific facts and philosophical conceptions whenever, and insofar as, they have admitted the lens of a creative world process.

So, then, what is Whitehead's constructive understanding of religion? Religion, for Whitehead, is that creative experiential process by which humanity is born as humanity. Religion functions as cultural elicitor of, as educational foundation for, civilization, as process of individuation, and of the unfolding of the aesthetical, rational, and spiritual universalization of the human mind/spirit, as well as the motor for societal and political developments. What these associations do not mean is that religion was not always equally able to undermine all of these processes. Religion can also be(come) a destructive force arguably unparalleled by any other force because of the unique energy it harbors and releases in human affairs. Yet, those fragmentations are, for Whitehead, secondary processes, based on the more fundamental insight that every creative process is able to mutate into a destructive form.

Religion emerges when the powers of fate and repetition (of cause-and-effect short circuits) give way to potentials for valuation and decisions, and achieve a creative freedom that cannot be reduced to the necessities of the biological life. Here, in the question of the origin of religion, Whitehead differs markedly from the proponents of the critique of religion (*Religionskritik*) at the turn to the 20th century. Instead of situating the natural emergence of religion (religious experience) in the context of a lack—the lack of resources, of social opportunities, of political freedom, of economical oppression, and so on—Whitehead among a very few (George Bataille comes to mind) understands the situation of the arising of religiosity (or spirituality) within a broader evolutionary process of hominization through the emergent appearance of an excess of energy. It is in the midst of the evolution of complex living societies (even of animals), as they begin to produce an excess of free energy beyond the necessities of survival (of food and shelter), that humanity, which is born from this situation, is capacitated also to communicate and celebrate the excess of free energy as potentials for cultural and ceremonial celebrations. In this process, humanity is constituted by, and gains, the capacity to find itself in enough critical distance from the natural and social definitions and limitations of survival so as to be able to creatively transform them. This

65

again, in Whitehead's view, furthered the emergence of the capacity for rationality, the understanding of the causal network in which an individual or a society is imprisoned as in a mere environment (*Umwelt*), but now (with this new capacity) can transcend into a *world* (*In-der-Welt-Sein*) beyond the limitations of its internal causal affairs. Note that, for Whitehead, the human (and humanized) world is generated by this creative emergence of, and transformation toward, aims (purposes, intentions, goals) and insights into their potentials (ideas, thoughts, ideals, visions, expectations). As all of these forces begin to serve the art of life (not only of survival, but of the good and the better life), this process begins to also free humanity in its depth (its soul) from the "heard psychology" of simplistic cultic and orthodox repetitions of religious tribalism, and widens its experiential potential into, and between, both the experience (and understanding) of the internal uniqueness of human existence (solitariness) and the external universality of the world (world loyalty). In this sense, Whitehead thinks of religious experience not as secondary reactions to some kind of lack, but as deep recognition of reality (of and beyond ourselves) and the highest unfolding of the uniqueness of the creative happening within our (or any) experience. And the human acts that recognize themselves in the fullness of their relationality answer the intuition of the universality of experience in the widest possible perception (prehension) of the potentials of the cosmos. Hence, for Whitehead the intellectual and creative power of religion for the art of human life lies in an insight that is formed by the unique, sublime, and irreplaceably singular "revelations" in which the world as a whole becomes visible in its fundamental relations.

This constructive proposal harbors an important implication for any current religious discourse on the basis of Whitehead's insight. Because of the unique character of such "events of revelation," there is (and can be) only a multiplicity of religions. They collect themselves genuinely around such figures in which they become excessively expressed—Whitehead mentions the Buddha, Prometheus, Moses, Jesus, and Mohammad—and around the free energy released by their experiences so as to crystalize themselves in historical fidelity to them, but develop creatively throughout the changes of time. It is, therefore, incumbent on philosophical theology to unfold itself in the multiplicity of these singular manifestations of the universal texture of the world without coming to be trapped within the delusion of only *one* orthodox representation of this universality or, in Eurocentric hubris, to claim its "neutrality" for the whole of humanity, which is often only a reiteration of one's preference for one's own religious roots. Moreover, such a process metaphysics knows itself in its theological implications a priori obligated to a multireligious manifold as well as it does readily acknowledge its inherent religious pluralism. It also knows of the incompleteness of its rationality and its openness to a "surrationality" of cosmic creativity in its irreplaceable appearances (revelations) in ever-new events and societies indebted to these events (as they not only allow an understanding of life, but also empower the living out of the potentials of their meaning). Only then will the aspiration for the harmonization of science, philosophy, and religion become possible and effective in composing new and peaceful modes of civilization.

Exploration 4

THE BIFURCATION OF NATURE

ONE OF THE MOST important insights of Whitehead's philosophy of science was to understand the limitations of the scientific method as being directed by its theoretical presuppositions, its philosophical outlook, and its ideological interests. In a long discussion of these limitations and their devastating consequences in *Science and the Modern World*, Whitehead reconstructed the history of the emergence of scientific materialism up to the late nineteenth century. Not only was it based on the introduction of the scientific method of empiricism from the seventeenth century on. It was already the outcome of a philosophical reaction against the religious and philosophical integralism of the European Middle Ages as well as the internal breaking apart of its holism. Against Plato's realm of ideas, which seems to have reduced *this* world to a shadow, this physical world now became the (only) valuable reality, to be understood not by means of divine revelation and the authority of the sages of old, but by a direct access through empirical experiments and theories of our own. Against Aristotle's empirical investigations, which had already made part of this move away from Plato, the new method also excluded any reverence for divine causality and an influx of nonempirical categories such as an inherent teleology of existing things. Things became matter. The ancient atomists, who had no need for either God or a creative internality of things, prevailed. Instead of the divine mind, the human mind became the measure of reality (as it had been for Protagoras). The sophists came back. But ironically, their relativism was to overturn even the anthropocentric implications of the scientific endeavor in a drive moving toward postmodernity. Descartes tried to hold these now-divorced spheres of mind and matter together, only to contribute to the dismissal of the mental side, as it was becoming reconstructed as illusion of movements of mere matter. Spinoza and Leibniz tried to circumvent this dualism with their respective monism of divine substance, being identical with the world, and pluralism of monads in the monad of God. But God had died with Nietzsche, Feuerbach, and Marx, and matter reigned in all quarters over and against mind, spirit, consciousness, values, God, and religion. It still tolerated art as a means and aim for a good life, but it lost humanity.

Whitehead saw the fatal flaw become obvious in the inconsistences of the ideology of division behind the scientific method, the philosophical antagonisms of empiricism and rationalism that underpinned it, and in their limitation vis-à-vis the new scientific insights and the shock coming with relativity theory and quantum physics. He captured this flaw with the term "bifurcation of nature." It is commonly assumed that Whitehead's with this phrase signals the split between mind and matter against which he wanted to demonstrate their presupposed interrelationship and that their divorce results in philosophical and scientific inconsistencies. While this is not wrong, it is nevertheless a simplification of matters. While it is true that Whitehead emphasized an *organic* conception of reality over against materialism, even within the sphere of scientific inquiry, and certainly in the philosophical integration of extension with internality in every event, his new concentration on events tried even more: to avoid not only materialism, but also any form of vitalism still pervading the philosophy, for instance, of Henri Bergson's *élan vital*, and to demonstrate that process and relationality are the key to either, in their denigration, making bifurcating dualism almost unavoidable or, in their recognition, being able to avoid it completely. In *Science and the Modern World,* he names this position still "organic mechanicism" in order to signal his aversion against the vitalism of a free floating life-force. But this phase in his thought was just the beginning of the introduction of metaphysics and divinity to address the implications of non-bifurcation. In *Process and Reality*, Whitehead's "philosophy of organism" develops fully the conceptual universe of a multiplicity of coherently related dualities instead (Sphere I). Yet, all began earlier, with his quite different introduction of the concept of the bifurcation of nature in *The Concept of Nature* (1920).

In this earlier rendering of bifurcation, Whitehead was not interested in the integration of mind and matter, but in the integrity of nature without reference to mind. What he wanted to avoid was to split *nature*, not an exclusion of the mind. We can understand what he means at this point in four steps: first, he wanted to differentiate a homogeneous understanding of nature, derived from its inherent elements, from a heterogeneous understanding that adds thought to nature. What we think *about* nature is not an element *of* nature as it appears from itself. Hence, the introduction of thought into the sphere of nature would produce the bifurcation to be avoided. Second, thought about nature is not meaningless, but excluded and reserved for an encompassing theory of nature *and* mind, which would be the business of a "metaphysical synthesis"; yet, that was not his intention at this point. His later work can, indeed, be understood as programmatic expansion of what he left open in his philosophy of science at that time: the inclusion of thought and mind, aesthetic and ethical values. Third, bifurcation is avoided if we try to know nature from its own constituents. But these must include the fact that nature always is already only in itself happening in relation to its perception. Perceptual events are moment of nature's own working and we cannot abstract from them. Fourth, nature must be understood as a relational complex of events in processes of perception, which again account for the creative passage of nature.

The homogeneous understanding of nature before any bifurcation, as Whitehead reconstructs it, presents nature with two necessary elements: the whole of nature as a fact and the parts of nature within this fact as a whole. Factors of the fact are related elements, relations within the whole really, which cannot be isolated from it without becoming something else: entities. Entities are factors of nature transformed into elements of thought instead of nature. This is the crucial step, the very transformation through which the bifurcation happens because of the heterogeneous introduction of mind. This is also the point where a certain philosophy has become the invisible motor for the bifurcation that, at the same time, as such became the scientific understanding of the world. Why? Because in the medium of thought, at least mediated through Greek philosophy, "matter" was constructed as consisting of self-contained entities in the container of an empty space, hurling through an absolute time frame. While factors are relational events, entities are isolated atoms. While the events relationships include perceptivity, material things exclude them as "secondary qualities"—for instance, denying the redness of the sun in the morning to be a perceptual factor of nature, instead making it just an illusion of measurable wavelengths.

In Whitehead's analysis, this bifurcation is at once the loss of relationality as it is the construction of substances. It is the loss of relationality insofar as thought constructs isolated entities from these relations. It is the construction of substances insofar as these abstractly constructed entities, which are really figments of the intervening mind, now pose as if they were the substrate for the relational factors making up nature as substance, transforming the relations that were the very basis for this move, to the mere qualities of themselves as substances. The bifurcation is perfect: the relational complex of nature with its perceptual qualities and its event structure has become a colorless and unperceptive, numb and blind, meaningless hurling of particles through the dark night of emptiness.

On the same basis (of the reversal of this bifurcation), Whitehead later expanded the relational event structure to include the mind, thought, aesthetics, and ethics. Making good on the promise to develop a metaphysical inclusion of elements of thought, we can understand his "metaphysics of experience" as exhibiting the same fundamental elements. First of all, no event is just where it is, but, like an energy field, somehow everywhere. Hence, all events are modulations of relations that are inherent to their unity as finite atoms of becoming. Second, all events are perceptual realties, experiences, connected through prehensive internalization and vector transition to new experiences based on their decisions. Third, all events are aesthetic realities of feeling and their transmissions. Consciousness and emotions are such modes of feeling—related to certain complex arrangements of events into societies and nexuses. Fourth, bipolarities of internal and external, subjective and objective, insistent and in-sistent, becoming and perishing, concrescent and transitional oscillation avoid the bifurcating reduction of reality into dualistic spheres of existence, like that of nature and thought. Humanity is now part of nature, as nature exhibits all the elements of mind as potentials of becoming.

Whitehead has described the bifurcation process as intrusion of unrelated interests of thought into nature with two famous fallacies. The "fallacy of simple location" captures the transmutation of relational factors into isolated entities and, at the same time, demonstrates that the scientific presuppositions of matter, how to understand it, and how to methodologically handle it, was itself based on a philosophical error: the substantialization of reality of independent entities with an essence and changing qualities. The wider "fallacy of misplaced concreteness," of which the former one is an application, reveals the most profound basis for this bifurcation process: that we (in our thoughts, theories, philosophies) tend to isolate entities from a vast background of interrelated events, nexuses, and societies of nature, the universe, or the cosmos—mostly because our mind needs to simplify what it wants to understand—and then forget that they are abstractions from reality. Instead, we make them the more real reality of the relational complexes we are to weak to grasp. In a hilarious confirmation and reversal of Plato, abstractions have again gained the status of a higher reality (like the Platonic Ideas), but now under the arbitrary denial of mental reality (while still using the mind to create these abstractions) reduced to dull mindless matter (whatever that is). What is more, we have used these abstractions (which are a product of imaginative mind) to tell us that there is no mind and, at best, that it must be seen as an illusion of combinations of elementary particles.

It is at this point that we can begin to understand how important the revolution in physics at the turn of the 20th century was for Whitehead. For his dissertation, Whitehead had already studied the electrodynamic field theory of James C. Maxwell. The impossibility to hold on to the ir-relational reductionisms of matter and even their mental dullness, given relativity theory and quantum physics, was just a last confirmation that the philosophy presupposed in the development of the scientific method was breaking apart on its own terms, in the experiments that lead to its self-refutation. Instead, now one could again begin to talk of the relativity of space-time and the probabilities of field particles in quantum states. In the end, in his book *The Function of Reason,* Whitehead even widens this view to evolution theory by understanding the mechanisms of the evolutionary process of biological organization as mechanistic reductionism from the creativeness of life—something today many biologists begin to see, too.

Exploration 5

SYMBOLISM

WHILE THE NEXUS OF events exhibits a prehensive structure, higher organizations of societies of events exhibit the
ability of perception. Perception is a complex form of organic orders and nested societies, holding together as concrete living organisms, to perceive other organisms through
organs of perception, like the sense organs. But Whitehead
will insist that it is not only sense perception that conveys
reality "out there" to us, but that in the evolution of complex organisms different modes of perception developed
without ever losing the fundamental prehensive structure
of their nexic relationship to the world beyond themselves.
Living bodies are more than perceptions, but they are—internally and externally—always connected through them.
Even when they develop emotions and consciousness,
mind and reason, these features are still integrated with
their perceptual and prehensive basis. What is more, these
connections express themselves in symbolisms, directly

being a consequence of these structures and being exhibitive of their very existence. In nuce, without such symbolic relations no understanding of the world we live in can be achieved or, conversely, without them neither reason nor experience, neither body nor mind are operative.

Whitehead's theory of perception—especially as developed in his book *Symbolism* (1927) and in parts of *Process and Reality*—and the resulting theory of symbolism must be situated in the discussion of the philosophical bifurcation between empiricism and rationalism in modern philosophy and its inherent dualism as a factor in the genesis of scientific materialism. While Descartes' dualism, in consequence, helped to show the irrelevance of mind for the understanding of the causal, and causally closed, reality of matter, so furthered Hume's equation of empirical experience with sense perception to define the method to investigate the physical realm through scientific means without recurs to secondary qualities. The scientific experiments were extensions of sense perceptions, and in this mode of experience we only know of physical causes and effects, their subjective impressions, like colors, only being illusions or, well, secondary phenomena that can be reduced to their primary physical sense contacts and integrations in sense organs as well as in the brain.

We have already seen how Whitehead deconstructs this setup as being based on a silent presupposition of substantialism (Exploration 4). But Whitehead goes even further and demonstrates that the same reversal of substituting the more primitive and actual with the more developed and abstract operates as the basis of this error of misplaces concreteness regarding perception. The extraction of scientific data from sense data presupposes—in substantialist manner—that the only things we can know about the world are the mere objective data inherent in perceptions: quantities of measurable mathematical objects gleaned from physical objects. In some theories, such as relativity theories, they can even be reduced to mere mathematical objects of the dimension of points, that is, without any extension. In other cases, they exhibit only mathematical equations of causal relations. We know, of course, that this already presupposes that concreteness could be stripped of any becoming, any event structure, any internality, and any prehensibility. Hence, Whitehead claims that the major move towards the materialist or physicalist reductionism is based on the assumption that sense perception is the originary mode of perception, the only one, and that the concreteness of secondary qualities, of subjective experiences, and mental attributes is just supervening on them through some mysterious accident.

The error of misplaces concreteness, here, consists in a more primitive mode of perception that actually exhibits secondary qualities, feelings, subjective experiences, and mental attributes falling into oblivion. Hence, Whitehead restores the supervening illusion back to its basic importance by differentiating from the elaborate mode of sense perception, called the mode of "presentational immediacy," that of the underlying prehensive organism, called "causal efficacy." The causality of this mode is, of course, not that of the effective causality in the physicalist sense, but that of the prehensive vector character of any event to any other by which it receives not just eternal objects, patterns, mathematical relations, and energetic forces, but a *feeling* of this object, a tone, a subjective form of transmission. And this causal efficacy does not immediately transmit forces like one billiard ball to another, but unites them in a creative act of self-concrescence with its cloud of potentials to a new creature before superjectively transcending itself into a new world it has helped to create.

Whitehead is somehow undecided on the origin of the two modes within the evolution of higher organisms, but sees presentational immediacy arising at a point where it contributes to the advance of organism to develop further into more intense forms of existence. This mode, in principle, is an advance, because it allows an organism not only to feel the myriads of feelings in a transmission of the past into the future, that is, in a temporal manner, but also to conceive of the contemporary present outside of the organism's direct causal contact. This again allows an organism to "present" to itself the experience of the world as a whole, and all organisms acting in it become contemporary actors to which an organism now can relate preemptively, before causal contact. This, finally, helps its survival, in a Darwinian sense, and the pursuit of a better, more intense, life through the newly won ability to create images, conceptions, and theories of the world and its position in it.

Moreover, in organisms that exhibit both modes strongly, as higher animals and humans do, this understanding leads to another surprising implication: that these two mode perceive the world in different ways—one as causal feelings of the past, the other as presentations of an immediate world as a whole—such that what they report to the perceiver must be coordinated. This is the birth of symbolism. The representation of one mode to the other is symbolic as one perception of reality is transferred to the other. All higher organisms exhibit this symbolic relationship to the world; and the more they do, the more they create symbolic systems in expression of their worldview, such as language, art, reason, and religion. In other words, presentational immediacy helps to develop the powers of the mental pole of integrated organisms to exhibit itself as one self-presence, consciousness, reflection, and mind. Since the symbolic reality in these organisms remain bound to the transfer of both more primitive modes into one another, mind, consciousness, complex emotions, reason, art, and religion always remain bound to the causal efficacy of bodily existence, that is, they never fall apart into independent spheres in any dualistic manner—similarity as the two poles of its events never disengage from one another. Mind and body, says Whitehead, are mutual pollutants. And a delineation of the boundaries between mind and body become only a matter of "pure convention."

Of the many interesting ramifications of this complex reality of symbolism, I will name only four. First, truth is not a matter of literalism, but of symbolism. Since the symbolic transfer between the two modes of perception is not fixed, that is, it is in some sense arbitrary. Predating the postmodern theories of Luce Irigaray and Julia Kristeva, we are not imprisoned in any symbolic system as if reality would be cut off from reality like Kant's mind. It is *because* of the presymbolic reality of the two modes of perception that this freedom prevails without becoming isolated from its basis. Yet, it is up to the decision of the organism in which mode it sees the meaning and in which mode the symbol. So can, to use one of Whitehead's examples, for common sense a tree be the meaning of the symbol "tree." But for a poet the mythological richness of "tree" can become the meaning for which a real tree is the symbol. This insight is of great importance for the understanding of religious symbols as they can only claim truth to the extent that this transfer is successful, which cannot be known beforehand, but must always be tested by experience.

Second, although Whitehead thinks both modes of perception within the symbolic transfer cannot be isolated and experienced in their "purity," he gives examples of an overwhelming emphasis of one mode over the other as the reason for certain existential moods of experiencing. If presentational immediacy overwhelms, one could experience a relaxation of the causal nexus, the history and context in which an organism is always immediately situated, and a feeling of emptiness can prevail (one is immediately reminded of the Buddhist *sunyata*). On the other hand, in the moments when causal efficacy seems to prevail, we might either feel our connectedness with the humming world of events that constitute us or the fear of haunting ghosts (one is reminded of *samsara* or *pratitya-samutpada*). In my own reading, these emphases connect with different mystical modes of experience. When, in the mode of presentational immediacy, Whitehead says, we experience the world "as one," we might think of the *unio mystica*, while in the mode of causal efficacy we might experience the karmic or demonic impossibility to escape the haunting past, or, conversely, to feel ourselves essentially as waves in a sea of creatures.

Third, since symbolic transfer needs experience to be tested, the truth of our theories about the world—religious or otherwise—are embedded in a pragmatism of "happiness," that is, we must test whether or not our assumptions will lead to successful reactions of the environment we live in. Hence, Whitehead's theory of symbolic transfer is a theory of environmentalism: only if we are able to create symbolic transfers that are sensitive to the societies of organisms we live in and with, which is the cosmic environment of our existence, will we be able to survive. Our environmental embededness needs our feeling of the world beyond ourselves and a presentation of it that feels its complex life of which we are an inextricable part. Hence, Whitehead ends *Symbolism* with an ecological prophecy: nature will not care if we die from the arbitrary imputation of unsuitable characters; but, contrarily, with an elaborate system of symbolic transfer we might achieve miracles of sensitivity to distant environments and to a problematic future.

Fourth, symbolic transfer is of eminent importance for (human) society as it lives from symbolic representations of its values and modes of interaction. As with the dipolarity of order and novelty in general, if a symbolic system becomes repetitive, that is, without reviving elements of novelty, the social order it represents will freeze and give way to revolts against its dead body. Conversely, the breakdown of a symbolic system—such as has happened, for instance, in the French Revolution—is always a highly unsettling and chaotic event in which only a new symbolic system can guaranty survival. Therefore, any order must always anew balance out with novelty. It is, for Whitehead, the first step in sociological wisdom to recognize that any major advance in civilization is a process that wrecks the society in which it occurs. This is all the more true for the history of religions. We must always anew decide between the havoc of the new and the atrophy of slow decay (Exploration 13). Hence, religious symbolism, as much as social symbolism, can never stay the same, but its change should follow the prophecy of ever-new successful symbolic transfers of its truths (Exploration 16). It is through such "change"—Whitehead insists on as being essential to religion as it is to science—we may gain evermore sensitivity to the even faint environments we finds ourselves in and the unknown future we want to welcome as creative realization of a divine manifestation of harmony and intensity.

Exploration 6

RELIGIONS IN THE MAKING

WHITEHEAD'S THEORY OF RELIGION is complex and distributed among his later works. But one characteristic is evident from his analysis of a creative cosmos of processual relationality: religion has an evolution; and its history must be one of a change of its symbolisms (Exploration 5). In fact, religion can only exist in the multiplicity of religions since nowhere in Whitehead's thought can unity stop process, and unification will always lead to a new multiplicity (Exploration 15). It is one of the distinctive features of Whitehead's access to religion that he thinks of it not as a desire that counters a lack (of economic means, social reconciliation, suppressed sexual desires, the missing security of a "strong man"). Rather, it is an expression of creative becoming, a manifestation of the spiritual implications of the processual relationality of reality. In religions, humanity realizes the deepest implication of its existence as self-conscious minds in an ecological embodiment. Religion is the means for a symbolic sensibility to an inherent spiritual dimension of the cosmic forces as they construct a universe. It allows for devolution into the brute force of literal truth claims, becoming a shell for self-interest and power struggles, but also for the realization of the non-violent intercommunication of mutual immanence. It is the appeal to a dimension of all experience that reveals the Good, but also to exceptional experiences in which this Good manifests itself in aesthetic seduction to self-transcendence through the organic realization of a civilization of peace, the development of the inherent potentials for the realization of some kind of a "kingdom of heaven."

In his book *Religion in the Making*, Whitehead formulates his first "theological synthesis" by following the traces of the emergence and development of religion as phenomenon, of types of religion, and of religion's metaphysical relevance. Here are four of the characteristics of its emergence, its constitution, and meaning. First, since, for Whitehead, religion is not (as in nineteenth-century *Religionskritik*) emerging from a human situation of lack that could be healed (through human endeavors) so that we could also be saved from religion's persistence, the reason for its arrival is connected with the emergence of human nature as such. We have already seen that the evolution of any type of organism is due to the organic organization of creativity. When organisms develop the ability to free their selves from the bare necessities of survival within their environment—such as food and shelter—the creative excess of free energy to use their day for something else creates the condition of a free reflection on this life of necessity. It is with this excess that culture becomes possible, that things begin to exhibit values beyond their mere utility, that celebrations of life become the first appearance of self-consciousness. Hence, Whitehead understands the emergence of religion as essentially connected to the ability of artificiality, the use of energy in a non-necessary way. In this, Whitehead grounds consciousness and culture, ritual and cult: to celebrate in memory the necessities of life from which one is liberated, but not excused. In this sense, the first appearance of religion happens in ritual celebrations of the self-consciousness of existence.

Second, Whitehead describes the evolution of religion in *four stages*. The first stage of ritual celebrations infuses new forms of feeling of intensity. Hence, the second mode of religion is that of the intensification of feelings induced by rituals. Emotional intensity again demands repetition and elaboration. Its repetition develops in evermore elaborate ritualistic activities and symbolizations. And, as a third stage, it gives way to elaborations of the symbolisms used in the celebrations by crating symbolic systems of belief. Beliefs again reinforce and creatively change the rituals and symbolism, now, not only anymore to heighten emotions through them, but also to understand the world in which the individual lives and the society reinforces itself as different from the necessities of life. The liberation from the necessities of life and nature that allowed the first manipulations of the life world of such a society and of the individual in it demands an understanding of its existence, origin and future. This is the birth of mythologies, of stories of the birth, development, status, and future of the world, one's society and one's situatedness in it. Finally, as a fourth stage, the emerging of the self-reflecting ability not only circles back to express a new ritualistic celebration reflecting the mythological findings, and this feedback not only heightens again the intensity of feelings, but it also leads to the liberation of rationality. "Rational religion" emerges. It integrates feeling and knowledge into a universal horizon of reflection that again can question the limitations of the mythological beliefs.

In order to better understand this fourfold developmental scheme, a few comments are in order. All religions today (of which we know) exhibit all four phases; that is, Whitehead is not claiming that some religions are only the expression of some of these elements, or are more primitive than others, or further back in their development. On the contrary, Whitehead emphasizes that there is no internal reason that these elements could not have arisen in a different order or together at once. The only two restraining features are: that the development of language and consciousness must allow for the unfolding of universal worldviews (rationality); and that the emergence of religion as ritual of free energy has occurred already in animals of which we cannot easily state the later phases. What is more, differences between religions will be contingently traditional, that is, arising from the inherently *local* diversity of the content of the four levels; and this will allow for varying *emphases* on one or the other stage, but will be always changing with the mutual feedbacks of their insights.

Third, the intention of the "rationality" of religion must not be confounded with "rationalism." To the contrary, this rationality expresses the ability to formulate a coordinated worldview of all elements of experience, which is in itself an aesthetic process that cannot be confined to logical consistency. Hence, Whitehead differentiates *three layers* inherent in all (rational) religions that will help to understand the paradox in the concept of a rational religion. Again, we find a combination of stations and developments of religions. All (rational) religions arose from a social organization, as this was the basis for the first three phases of ritual, emotion, and mythology. But in the emergence of universal reflection on the world as a whole, the identity of a religion, with its local society becomes profoundly relativized from two sides: from *within* a universal worldview and from a world that can be *travelled* so as to realize different social and religious organizations and worldviews as relevant and potentially viable as alternatives. This discrepancy between local society and universality of the world, again, forces a profound wedge between the individual and its society; it may even be instrumental in the appearance of individuality (in the full sense of a free, responsible, consciously and reasonably deciding subject of its actions). Hence, the age of "rational" coordination of all elements of experience regarding the universe as a whole as the imminent horizon of reflection also creates, paradoxically, a marked independence of the newly (by it) constituted individual in this universal horizon and, hence, its growing independence from the society and its religious expectations one was born into or is integrated.

The implications are enormous: the age of religious "relationality" creates martyrs, says Whitehead. As the individual becomes independent from the limitations and necessities of tribal boundaries, the discovery of a universal horizon of religious experience, reflection, and existence also becomes a means of the discovery of solitariness. With William James, Whitehead conforms to one definition of religious existence concerned with the inner solitariness of the individual. Yet, he immediately adds another one: religion is concerned with world loyalty. The liberation from the "herd psychology" that this development in the phase of rational religion implies becomes Whitehead's icon for *truly* religious experience and demonstrates his opposition to sociological explanations of religion. Religion does, in its depth, not arise as long as it is bound by the limits of contingent societies and their way of life—it is not the expression of its status quo and the justification of the powers to uphold it. Rather, religion arises (only) when solitariness and world solidarity overcome these limitations and expose the depth of their paradoxical contrast. Hence, Whitehead finds the most important expressions of religious existence in the scenes of (universally relevant) solitariness that haunt the imaginations of civilized humankind. In Whitehead's words: Prometheus chained on the rock, Mohammad brooding in the desert, the meditations of the Buddha, and the solitary man on the cross. In fact, the spirit of religious experience comes into its own when it expresses Godforsakenness.

Fourth, contrasted with the aloneness is the rise of metaphysics, the understanding of experience in the context of universal reflection on the world as a whole. Whatever suggests cosmology, suggests religion, Whitehead remarks. And what suggests the religious importance of this arrival of metaphysical universality is, again paradoxically, that its rationality is interrupted by the "surrationality" of the depth of the religious spirit. Therefore, Whitehead admits that religious experiences of this kind, although they may be a rare appeal to special events (and for many of us only accessible through extraordinary figures in which they dwell in their raw form), have elucidatory power for the nexus of events that is the universe and its philosophical understanding. Universal religions, then, always exhibit a metaphysical dimension that derives from the extraordinary experiences of humanity arising in the moments of its finest insights.

This, of course, from the perspective of a metaphysics of experience, implies that there will always be, and in fact there always was, a multiplicity of unique experiences of the most sublime kind that gave rise to different religious systems, or the worldview of different religious traditions, which are at their core somehow bound by these events of their origination throughout their further development. It also implies that the philosophical endeavor is a natural and unavoidable part of religions and their self-constitution as unique expressions of the world as a whole. Then again, it implies that there can neither be only a single metaphysics nor any finally closed model for its rationality.

A final thought: for the future of religions, Whitehead's theory of the becoming of religions offers some interesting perspectives. Religions, as long as they are contrasting solitariness and world solidarity, must understand themselves in the world as a whole, yet being a unique expression of events of exceptional depth, and to act accordingly. As a symbol of the plurality of philosophical (rational) universality and religious (experiential) uniqueness and, maybe, as symbolic limits of the whole landscape, Whitehead emphasizes three traditions of cosmological relevance in relation to religious interpretation: Christianity, Buddhism, and—surprise!—science. Not only does Whitehead see them compete among themselves for the truth of their interpretations; they also demonstrate that it is not about certain doctrines—for instance, whether there is a God or not—that defines their cosmological views to prevail, but about the plurality of traditions they hide (Exploration 14). Maybe, then, the future becoming of religions, or that which suggests cosmology, is about the mutual immanence of their respective experiences and their peaceful coordination beyond any claim of superiority and exclusiveness.

SPHERE III

GOD AND COSMOS IN CREATIVE MUTUALITY

IF YOU HAVE FOLLOWED the argumentation up to this point, then the first two Spheres should have made clear that Whitehead's concept of God pervades the complexities of the elucidation of the relational web of world processes and their creative reconstruction in the triangle of science, philosophy, and religion enabling it to serve the unfolding of a civilizational dynamic. It is also important to recognize that for Whitehead the philosophical conception of divine reality does not want to claim any preference for a specific religion (except that there are only specific religious experiences leaning themselves to the origination of a multiplicity of religions). Nor does Whitehead's approach imply the unreserved approval of any orthodoxy of a specific religion, not only because any religion would in itself harbor another multiplicity of conceptual formulations of specific experiences, but because such experiences always resist dogmatic reductions to sedimented formulations.

Even if it may be fair to observe that the history of the reception of Whitehead's "theology" has, at first glance, mostly developed in the sphere of influence of Christianity—which has, at times, led to a vague identification of process theology with a specific form of Christian theology—this is by no means a necessity conjunction, but remains a contingent fact of its historical locality. Today, however, it is not at all the case that Whitehead's "process theology" is limited to the Christian realm (nor has it ever been in a genuine sense), nor that it could only prove itself viable under the preconditions of Christian doctrine (not that standing such a test would be a bad sign for anything either). Whitehead himself has readily acknowledged this contingency of the religious commitments of his thought and has situated the "question of God" in a complex interreligious landscape with its divergent experiential multiplicities and conceptual diversifications. This should not hinder us to embrace the rich history of the interaction of Whitehead's thought with Christianity and, more generally, occidental theological forms of thought and their philosophical siblings, which actually do occur in his work. But it should warn us to identify the motivation of Whitehead's philosophical analysis of experience (and its inherent religious implications) with his respect for the revelatory uniqueness of such experiences as, for instance, constitute Christianity.

Hence, in *Religion in the Making*, Whitehead consciously tries to avoid any rigid delimitation of his process approach to any specific communally necessitated restriction of identity (as specific religious identity of a tradition and of a society with its restrained characteristics seems to demand). He prefers open forms of a transgressing relationalism (and, hence, relativism) to any demand to neatly fit his "theology" into types of reflective religious identities like theism (with its transcendentalism), pantheism (with its acosmism), or cosmotheism (with its monism). He withholds judgment on whether God should be (more appropriately) viewed as person, which would obviously correlate more with the occidental religions of Abrahamic trajectories, or better should avoid personal categories entirely, as is ultimately the preference of the oriental religions of Dharmic and Daoist provenience. Moreover, Whitehead—most surprisingly (over against any reductionism slipping in by conceptual simplification)—interfuses the notion of "God" itself in the contrastive field of references to Christianity and Buddhism, which does not entertain any concept compatible with specific occidental concepts of God (except in their mystical sub-streams). And, finally, Whitehead posits all of these provisions so as to avoid being misunderstood in his *philosophical* choice of "divine" language and its implied transreligious dimension, that is, constituting philosophical theology always already as a multireligious discourse.

What is most surprising in this endeavor is the sheer fact that Whitehead—after the perceived "death of God" and the reductionist deconstructions of religion at his time—found himself in the same position as Aristotle who admits "God," not for any specific religious commitment, but because of a purely conceptual necessity—although now, in Whitehead's case, in the form of a God of/for becoming—into philosophical discourse. Wrapped in a grand paradox, Whitehead allows for the introduction of a divine sphere into philosophy in order to render *intelligible* the togetherness of all structural elements necessitated by a world of processual relationality in the contours of human experience—*and,* in turn, a world being conductive of a civilizational dynamics.

Indeed, in *Science and the Modern World* he conjures up the witness of Aristotle as the last philosopher (before Whitehead) who was not oriented toward, or led by, religious motives in developing a philosophical theology as an essential element of his metaphysics in order to render intelligent the fact that and how and why the world is *in movement*. As in Aristotle, God does not appear as a first cause being in a cause-effect relationship with the world, pushing the world into existence, but as the attractor that seduces the world into a becoming, transforming the inert into a potential for aiming (in all its diversity) at its perfection. In Whitehead's thought, God becomes the *eros* of the initiation of experiential existence and the seduction for a becoming of experience toward a state of satisfaction and the transformation beyond itself into the experiences of other events in becoming.

Such a metaphysics of experience must, therefore, be inherently open to religious experiences and conceptual renderings of its constituents that allow for religious connotations. Yet, at the same time, such universal patterns of experience must also allow for the fact that the concrete ways in which such experiences address their religious dimension inherently and structurally demand to transcend the metaphysical understanding that reveals its structural necessity. In other words, the universal pattern of experience in Whitehead necessitates the paradox that it can only be a fact of experience if it values its own uniqueness in the revelation of this pattern. In this sense, unique religious experiences and their conceptualizations are to be expected to constitute, no less than the surprising inescapability of revelatory events that transcend the generality of the metaphysical structure that accounts for their existence and detection. The important implication is this: revelation co-constitutes the metaphysical project.

It is at this point that a classical discussion about the potential sources of God-consciousness in the human world is addressed in a new way. While we find often a great amount of energy put into oppositions regarding the value of such sources—such as revelation versus experience, scriptural positivity versus mystic silence, relativism of diverse traditions of understanding versus immanent insight (beyond language), orthodoxy versus personal inspiration—Whitehead's paradox of uniqueness and universality tries to avoid, overcome, and integrate presupposed dualisms from the outset. Since all religious experience is a part of experience as such (that is, since there is a dimension of divinity within any experience in form of the initial *eros* of becoming subjects), the structure of experience always already includes any expression of it in more specific forms: mediated by language, ecstasy, or realization of virtues. Conversely, any specific expression can be unique (as it harbors such a novelty in contrast to the course of the world) in such a sense that it also manifests its specific *eros* as universal *logos*: as unique revelation in the course of the world that cannot be reduced to the structure it presupposes and out of which it arises, but still is of universal relevance. Although novelty is unprecedented, it can be resonant with the general pattern of experience, that is, it can be perceived, understood, and imitated. In this twofold function (not one without the other), events of revelatory novelty become the nucleus of religions in their diversity without—again following the principle already expounded—violating their unity in this diversification.

This metaphysics of experience can only actualize its essence in the space of the plurality of religions in a milieu in which it must itself allow to resonate, diversify, and gain insights beyond any generality of assumptions. In the end, as experience is only real in the multiplicity of experiences with their unique tone, and as creativity is only real in the multiplicity of its events, so can metaphysics only be real in the multiplicity of unique experiential revelations of the divine dimension of becoming as it instigates ever-new satisfactions of becoming—individual and social expressions of harmony and intensity. Religious identities, as they are circulating through the universal experiential structure of the universe, will find themselves among siblings, related to one another more deeply than any sense of misguided superiority might like, and can make, one believe.

In this move, we can recognize the congruence in Whitehead's thought pattern between the *ontological* categories of relation and process in the rhythmic gestalt of "creativity," namely, as renewal of a relationally brimming plurality with any newly constituted and self-transcending actual entities; the *epistemological* paradox, namely, that rational insight in the universal structure of the world process can only reach abstract generalizations, which are missing the uniqueness and dynamics of the figures of happening from which they are abstracted and which, hence, must be always made resonant with *their* dynamics (so as to not degenerate into mere abstractions); and the *theological* paradox, in which a philosophical concept of God cannot express generality unless it is not thoroughly dynamized by universalizations of unique religious experiences of and revelations about, the whole of the world in specific religions, but may not entrap itself or dissolve in them either.

The most profound features of Whitehead's understanding of the concept God result from the hitherto collected characteristics of its relativity to the analysis of (religious) experience. God does not signify an abstraction from relational processes, but is the quintessence of their potentiality and their healing transformation. God must, therefore, be understood in the image of an *actual* reality in which the characteristics of processual relationality must be fulfilled in a universal and universally relevant, but unique and distinctive sense. Hence, God neither names the Being of beings—a function that in Whitehead's metaphysical scheme is filled by creativity—nor a being among beings (or the highest being)—as in the onto-theological turn of occidental thinking. God calls to remembrance that the inter-net of relations of all happenings faces a future (an advent) by which every event in its uniqueness is called to novelty of existence (an adventure) through a sphere of potentials unique to its past. In other words: it is constituted by—what Whitehead calls—an "initial aim," a potential unity that is it origin "from a future" released by the *eros* of divine initiative. And as the other side of this adventure, when the event has become, is satisfied and has transcended itself into other actual worlds of not yet existent entities of becoming, God equally is the call to memory of this and all events as they disappear in their passage into the past. Since an event will only remain meaningful if it is available for further creative transformation, this past does realize itself in new events in the mode of heritage—the mode Whitehead calls the "objective immortality" of an event in others. But it is only if it is also perceived (prehended) in the memory of *that* event (God) that holds this sphere of possibilities open and available and turned toward the uniqueness of every new event, that its remembered immortality is of eternal importance. In other words, God is the event in which the unprecedented constellations of creative and destructive forces, which heighten or reduce the intensity of the dynamics of the relational inter-nexus, are processed as perceptions (prehension) of *this* event, because it alone can transform them *in itself* (in God) and release them (in transformed modes) again into the world process with the intention of the realization of ever-greater harmonies and intensities.

The immanence of God in the world process in every event is that of infinite enablement (possibility) of the creative renewal of the relational nexus of the world. In it, God calls to actualization the potentialities of any and every concrete (concrescent) happening. This aspect of God is, in Whitehead's terminology, the "primordial nature" of God. The transcendence of God, contrasting the world process, collective of all happenings, however, is that infinite relational space "in" God in which all realized events (actualizations of potentials) are perceived (prehended), set in mutual relation, and transfigured into a healing and healed form of wholeness. In Whitehead's terminology, this aspect of God is named the "consequent nature" of God.

It is in this cycle of the relational process in the oscillation of creative becoming between God and the world that God and the world are both in themselves and in relation to one another united and differentiated. Note, however, that this uniting and differentiating, oscillating and cycling movement never amounts to the confusion between God and the world. Neither is God only an expression of the cosmic form of relationality as God is inherently the fullness of all potentialities and actualities, nor is the world an instrument of the self-satisfaction of God as God's relational activity always purposes the harmony and intensity of the world process. Hence, if because of this oscillation God is never thought to be without a world, this can, then, by no means be taken as a sign that God is delimited, temporalized, naturalized, or bereaved of divine nature. It does not mean that God cannot really create, or only was a platonic demiurge that must presuppose material, or that God has become a finite player in the multiplicity of forces. Rather, we can now witness an abundance of relationality as God's "grandeur"—instead of the ability to be independent and "alone." This approach can also be seen as a new way to understand divine "power," namely, as the ability to call into existence novel relationships out of exhausted relationships, to call them beyond what was into unique existence, *and* to call them in their brokenness to wholeness and healing—instead of the ability to control, to rule with absolute force (to rule with violence), or to destroy (the power of annihilation). And this view signifies God's "infinity" in new and refreshing way as that of an infinite creativity that is also able to embrace and include in itself all happenings in order to transform them within a divine dynamics of life—instead of an impassibility, the characteristic not to be touched by the world. God, in this process understanding, is eternal and everlasting, beyond time and time-sensitive, infinite and embracing finitude. God and the world are in their own distinctive way creative, they embody in their own way unity and multiplicity, and they move in a mode of contrast counter to each other, toward each other, and in one another, unmixed and undivided. The conceptual expression with which Whitehead comprises these dynamic contrasts is *mutual immanence*—in a true sense *the* ultimate reality in Whitehead's thought.

We must not be astonished, therefore, that Whitehead uses this circular image of a processual movement of mutual immanence to indicate the interwoven nexus of the cosmos; or that this image indicates the mutual exchange of God and the world in a process of mutual novelty and healing. To the contrary, we can maybe understand better, now, why Whitehead is left with only one term to express this movement of inherent contrasts, namely: with the religious categories of creative and healing *love*. In fact, it is this love that enables Whitehead to interpret the totality of the process as the dynamics of creative configurations (through the initiatives of the primordial nature) and of their trans-figurations into the "heavenly kingdom" (through the pre-hension of the world into the consequent nature). It should also have become comprehensible, now, why Whitehead presents this exposition of the primordial rhythm of this abundance of relationality not under the oppressive weight of the notion of divine omnipotence. The all-potency of God is rather that of a love that instigates creativity beyond control and, at the same time, seeks to prevent anything from getting lost.

In an interesting turn against the whole occidental phil-osophical tradition to understand the nature of an *act* (and, hence, God's acting), Whitehead has reversed the force that tradition has lent to oppressive modes of power—be it in a physical, sociological, or theological sense. Whitehead does not picture the divine *act* under the archetype of *effective acting,* like an atomistic cause at its effects or as an external positing of things into nothingness beyond divine reality. To the contrary, in its most sublime form, activity is first and foremost *receptivity* (or responsiveness)—concrescing unification of/from diversity—that connects, brings forth, and seduces in tenderness toward harmony and intensity. It is with this antitype of divine acting that we have not only overcome the crude notion that the effectiveness of God in the world *must* be guided by the paradigm of the Meso-potamian emperor—in whatever subtle form imaginable. What is more, we have, thereby, already accepted a totally different paradigm of power: that of empowerment to the self-creativity of each and every creature; that of potentiza-tion to ever new relational configurations; that of healing transformation; that of imperturbable non-violence; that of the relevance of mutual in-being.

It is this paradigm that Whitehead sees to come to the front in the evolution of religions and as their true contribution to a maturated understanding of how to create a peaceful civilization of the future. This is the meaning of Whitehead's "process theology"—to function as philosophical medium in which the multireligious streams and traditions can recognize themselves in their unique contribution to such a civilizational endeavor. In this effort, it wants to offer a lens to the direction religions may take effect in this creative process; a lens through which the civilizational roots of the cosmos can become visible.

At this point, we must take Whitehead's critique of religion (*Religionskritik*) up again. In the passage through Whitehead's dramatic reconstruction and transformation of the conventional religious categories, which should *not* have found philosophical, spiritual, and theological applications in the first place, it has become a critique of theology. In his estimate, Whitehead counts among the greatest deformations of religious discourse, regardless in which religion it might arise, the *devolution* of unique experiences, of primal religious intuitions and the primal impulses released by them, *into* theological (and theologically justified) patterns of violence, control, and the legitimation of political power in the image of Caesar.

As long as we remain sensitive to the processual and relational analysis of (religious) experience (and any doctrine building on their uniqueness) as exhibiting the profound cosmic composition of the world, the accompanying religious discourse (theology) will not fall into the trap of isolation, superiority, supersession, and sectarian dogmatism. Instead, by recognizing (experiencing) the value of these primal impulses as expression of—and not as resistance to—their mediation through mutual immanence (although in always unique configuration), Whitehead's thought can guide us in a new theological discourse on our multireligious existences. It will point at the inherence of tender forces of transformation if we are willing to detect them. It will further the love not only for the eternal, but also for the impermanent appearances of creativity as they create a universe without which eternity was empty. It directs us away from separatism and damnation of the (perceived) other toward a universal prehension in which we can hope for the healing of brokenness, without the need to denigrate the relational and creative process of the world as a whole.

The enemy in this critique of theology is the all-too-human grasping of love in the image of fear in order to gain control over the masses by legitimizing the bid for synchronized language, a normalized economy of social structures and forms of thought. It is this gospel of fear—so prominent in Whitehead's analysis of theology—that converts the vital, vivid, and living experience of the divine into abstract metaphysical principles, control mechanisms of dishonest moralities, and a small-minded flight mechanism in the clutches of clerical potentates. It is this devolution to the "herd psychology," or the inability to overcome it, that Whitehead seeks to counteract with his philosophical wildfire so as to allow the new seed of a liberated ecological cross-fertilization of all with all to begin to bear its wondrous fruits.

Exploration 7

ULTIMATE REALITIES

TODAY, IN INTERRELIGIOUS DISCOURSES, the question regarding ultimate realities has become a standard feature, but also a problem. On the one hand, it is meant to neutralize the presupposition that only religious tradition that include a concept of God can participate, and on the other hand, it tries to capture the philosophical question of ultimacy inherent in religions. Generally, it will be wise to ask these questions regarding specific religious traditions so as not to assume a specifically structured ultimacy in the process of comparison between traditions. But the philosophical question, within and independent of religions, will try to answer this question for all religions, if it accepts them at all. So is, for instance, Heidegger's ground of Being and the question, "Why is there something rather than nothing?", not limited to any specific religious tradition, but would be valuable for the consideration of all of them as they venture in the inherently philosophical exploration of their experience. The dialectic between universality and uniqueness is unavoidable, but always problematic both in the internal application of certain philosophical models to religious traditions, as it already has implications for the understanding of all other traditions, as well as in the comparative application of the philosophical model as a matrix for the communication between religious traditions. This conundrum will be heightened by the fact that there will always only be a plurality of competing philosophical models for either process of application.

Whitehead can, of course, not escape this complex dilemma. The best he can do is to lay open the inner workings of his metaphysics of experience. Thereby, he exposes the transformative matrix of his own thought patterns to include philosophical rationality and uniqueness of events and experiences into one process of connectivity that is the universe. His metaphysical description begins with the becoming and perishing of the cosmos in all of its events, nexuses, and societies, and it asks for the constant elements in it that constitute this process as ultimately real and concrete. As all religious experiences, as well as scientific explorations, generated in this process ask for such structures, they are in this sense ultimate constants of becoming (since, if there was only becoming and perishing, there would neither be any natural laws nor any organisms related by patterns of persistence). Yet, insofar as Whitehead holds onto the process itself as the "creative passage of nature" of the universe we live in, such structures are, importantly, abstractions in the mental process of the understanding of this process. Hence, not only by the plurality of events, experiences, and rationalities based on them, but by the simplifications of the mind in its process of making things understandable, there remains an openness of the philosophical rendering of ultimacy to new insights, new events, and new experiences as of yet unknown. In fact, while it is true that Whitehead's universe was a grand paradigm shift from the analysis of the eternal constituents of the universe to the process of novelty as ultimate, as Gilles Deleuze has highlighted, Whitehead does not discard the eternal constants, but reinterprets them as abstractions of the process of the concrete reality itself—and in this sense as ultimate.

For these reasons, in *Religion in the Making*, Whitehead, acknowledging that there are many ways to analyze the universe regarding that which is comprehensive of all there is, employs two perspective to be able to penetrate deep down to its ultimate constituents: first, that the *actual* world is a creative passage, or better, temporality; and second, that the elements of world *formation* resist temporal deconstruction. Now, Whitehead uses an interesting instrument, namely, a matrix of (all) possible relationships between the constituent elements of analysis. These elements, hence, are: concrete actuality (concrescence) and temporality (transition). With their differentiation and negation, they form a matrix of all possible combinations: namely, the elements of becoming—actuality and temporality; and the elements of non-becoming—non-actuality and nontemporality.

There combination offers us these four elements of all becoming, being their ultimate realities: that which is actual *and* temporal—this is the world of events, nexuses, and societies; that which is non-actual *and* nontemporal—this is the cloud of eternal objects (possibilities, potentials, alternatives, ideas, forms, structures, patterns); that which is non-actual, *but* temporal—this is creativity, which is not an actuality (event), but the activity of all temporal actualities; and finally that which is actual, *but* nontemporal—that is God, the one nontemporal actuality. The actual realities are concrete, the non-actual realties are abstract; the temporal realities become and perish or are the internal ground for the creative passage, the nontemporal realties are constants providing becoming with their pattern of organization.

So, there are four ultimate realities in Whitehead's process analysis of existence, comprising the abstract and the concrete, the becoming and the eternal: the world, the realm of possibilities, creativity, and God. Although all of them are analytical abstractions, simplifications, arising from the way the concrete world of processual connectivity is analyzed, their matrix includes concreteness and abstraction as moments of the conceptual matrix in which, indeed, all that is, is captured. It is through this kind of conceptualization that Whitehead is able to connect with interreligious comparisons of diverse traditions whether they may be theistic or monistic, pantheistic, panentheistic or nontheistic. Several process authors have used this or a similar differentiation of ultimate realities to understand diverse religious leanings towards one or the other as expression of their unique religious experiences (Sphere IV). While Christianity, for instance, will generally highlight God over against creativity, Buddhism, for instance, might generally rather commit to immanent creativity than to a transcendent God.

Hence, process theologians have variously emphasized one or the other, reduced them to only some of them, or collapsed some of them. The more monistic and pantheistic streams of process thought have variously identified God and the world or God and creativity. Either God was dissolved into the network of becoming or into the reality of creativity. In both cases is the tendency one of dissolving the transcendence of God into the immanence of the relationality or the process of the world itself. More theistic tendencies among process thinkers have, conversely, led to strengthen the position of the transcendence of God in relation to the world by reabsorbing creativity back into God as the original creator. The aim was to make sure that God's creativity is not a natural necessity, but a (divine) gift of free will. Some others have tried to exploit instead the intercreativity, that is, the commonness of creativity to all actual entities—whether any event of the world or of the divine event—by identifying it with God in the function of non-dual indifference from the world and, hence, unite God as the personal side of divinity, with the nonpersonal side of divine activity in all happenings of the world (in an endeavor to intimate eastern religious sensibilities). Some others have tried to deconstruct not God and creativity (into one another), but specifically God *as* nontemporal entity (with its seeming atemporal stability), since, they say, Whitehead already includes God as the *process* of the imagination of new futures and the reception of actualized possibilities in concrete events, nexuses, and societies. Others again have tried to deconstruct Whitehead's cloud of possibilities, the eternal objects, which seems still too much a reminder of Plato's realm of Ideas.

In any case, we should be aware that these ultimate realities in Whitehead are only understood comprehensively if we see them rested in Whitehead's basic intuition of processual connectivity. Only then do we remain aware that in isolation they are abstractions from the concreteness of the nexus that is existence. Whitehead has, for this very reason, made clear in *Process and Reality* that God and the world are to be understood in mutual oscillation of their contrastive creativity. In this sense, mutual immanence is already the unnamed ultimate of ultimates in Whitehead's fourfold scheme (Exploration 10). Yet, even mutual immanence is nothing but an abstraction if it is substantialized beyond the relational process itself. However, as the medium it might be "more" ultimate than the realties appearing as its four "formative elements."

With this analysis of the formative elements of the world process (one might say, the multiverse), Whitehead has gained a powerful position to sustain the world process without beginning and end, but also without losing the ability to establish its ultimate factors as eternal. And he has demonstrated a point of access for the introduction of God into the analysis of the process without resorting to religious doctrines (but being explanatory of their relevance). What is more, a certain relationship between these ultimates in relation to the world process becomes visible: creativity and eternal objects, since they represent mere abstractions from the process, that is, are not actualities, provide infinite freedom and potentiality of becoming, but cannot act; God, on the other hand, is that actuality that can connect these infinities so as to provide structures, patterns, modes of intensity, and harmony for the process. Whitehead names this function of God the Wisdom of God, which, with the other infinities, remains eternally, but time-related—even if the world becomes a ripple indistinguishable from nonexistence in the vast infinity of the becoming of (new) worlds from which it has arisen by the wonder of God's aims of goodness, truth, and beauty.

Exploration 8

THE COINHERENCE OF
OPPOSITES

IN THE FINAL SECTION of *Process and Reality*, Whitehead
tries to integrate his metaphysical discussion of experience,
which had already included the primordial nature of God,
into the frame of a religious mind-set. As was already discussed at several points in this book, Whitehead's idea of
processual oscillation, in which no element can be abstracted from all others, but is always connected with all others
in a coherent way (in Whitehead's meaning), has led him to
speak of multiple forms of dualities in motion: of physical
and mental poles, of concrescence and transition, of becoming and being (perishing, being past), of one (unification)
and many (multiplication), of permanence and fluency. In
the final analysis, this leads to the two contrastive dualities
that comprise them of all: the first one by acknowledging
that God must be concrete, an actuality, not an abstraction

or a reason or a ground alone; the second one by discussing the relationship between God and the world. The former one is addressed by the differentiation between the primordial and the consequent nature of God—God's mental and physical pole; the latter one is addressed with a series of six antitheses in which God and the world are shown to be bound together in mutual creative oscillation. While all dualities are coinherences of opposites in concrete processes of mutual oscillation, their character comes to an eminent discussion in these two instantiations.

Although I will return to the first oscillation between the two natures of God and of them with the world in the next section (Exploration 9), insofar as it shares light on the creatures of the world involved here, it is interesting to register some of the more outstanding characteristics of this oscillation regarding the nature of God, here. First, God has not only a mental pole, but also a physical pole. This is an important statement of any event structure to make since without it no reality would be concrete. Hence, the relationality of the process does not stop short of expressing God's own being as supreme form of such a relational process or processual relationality. God is not conceived independently from a world of events to which God is essentially related. Second, in God's mental nature, God is, nevertheless, independent from the world since the primordial nature comprises all possibilities, ideas, patterns, structures, and forms (of becoming) insofar as they may be, but also may not be, may have been, may yet be, or not ever have been, involved in any particular process in the world. Here, God is understood as eternal, pretemporal, and independent of any happenings. But, at the same time, it symbolizes the wealth of the potential realizations of the world, an offering of a future, of novelty, of becoming, of the realization of the unprecedented. Hence, even in God's independent eternity, God is not just eternal, but God's eternality is the infinite potential of life for the world. Third, that God also exhibits a physical nature implies (and is implied by the assumption) that God prehends the actualities of the world. In this aspect, God is not "dependent" on the world (as classical theists would have it), but the everlasting integration of the world's harvest of actualization into God's sovereign actuality. Fourth, in both natures, God is divine, not mundane: neither does God change nor perish. In fact, both natures exhibit the power of the creative integration of divine concrescence: God's primordial nature is not only a pool of possibilities, but the divine process of valuation of all possibilities regarding each individual becoming event in the world. And God's prehensions of the world into God's consequent nature is not a data collection, but the "kingdom of heaven" in which God evaluates all that has become in light of the primordial Wisdom, as this Wisdom is already sensible to the actual needs of becoming by having perceived the heritage of any actual entity in becoming.

In consequence, the oscillation of the two natures of God includes the mutual immanence of them in one another *and* their indwelling in all events *as well as* the indwelling of all events in God. How can this be any deficit of eternity and sovereignty if it addresses a life abundant that does not have to reject becoming, perishing, even failure? In order to make sure that it is understood that God is not *literally* an event among events, Whitehead adds that God's becoming of the two natures is different from that of any event that constitutes the world. It is different in the sense that its permanence is of eternal power and infinite scope, while that of any event in the world is always finite and prone to perishing. Therefore, also God's flux is not that of any perishing event, but the highest expression of the infinite potentiality of God to heal and integrate despite all failings and shortfalls, evil and hindrances, of the event histories integrated. In fact, God's and the world's permanence *and* flux—we remember, these are the two elements Whitehead uses to analyze the process into ultimates (Exploration 7)— move contrary to one another. They are opposites in the movement of mutual coinherence.

This leads us to the other contrasted opposition, namely, that between God and the world in mutual creative oscillation. Whitehead addresses this final crowning integration of the dual character of all processual connectivity in six antitheses. Having integrated the cloud of potentials into the primordial nature, Whitehead still works from the fourfold ultimacy of *Religion in the Making*, but now concentrating on the concrete process of the mutual coinherence of God and the world in their intercreativity. In the unfolding of these antitheses, Whitehead uses the utmost oppositions used in classical metaphysics to characterize God and the world, respectively, in mutual exclusion to indicate the mutual *inclusion* of God and the world by way of the application of their seeming opposition as modes of a duality in oscillation between both God and the world. Hence, to use immanence and transcendence, one and many, permanence and flux, actual reality and creativity for both God and the world, is not only a coincidence of opposites (in a mystical sense), but their coinherence as dualities in their respective reality and in one another as mutual relatedness in process. This process again *is* creativity, which Whitehead in this context defines as the creative transformation of opposites—indicated with the utmost opposites of God and the world—into contrasts. "Contrast" is the category of mutual coinherence that characterizes processual relationality on every level. The creation of contrasts *is* the creative process.

Although the many spectacular implications of the final synthesis of the antitheses in the sixth, to which their whole dynamics converges, cannot be exhausted here, solely to present it will reveal its remarkable claim: *it is as true to say that God creates the world as it is to say that the world creates God.* Here ontology and epistemology converge. God's being is in becoming in relation to the world, as is the world in relation to God. But the God-creating world exhibits also no less than the possibility that we create God—but how: in our image, in our actualization, as reality, or as idea? What would be the implications for religious experience if God wanted it to be activated to become creative not only of an intense and harmonious world, not only of a kingdom of heaven, on earth or in God's consequent nature, but also of God's experience, concept, spiritual perception, actualization itself, of God Godself (Exploration 16)?

This mutual creative oscillation of God and the world provides also another take on the question of ultimate realities discussed before (Exploration 7), namely, *as* mutual coinherence. Given the renderings of diverse process thinkers of the mode of integration between ultimates that they either prefer philosophically or in their sensibility to diverse religious tradition, it seems that the mutual oscillation of ultimates is *immersed* in the perspective from which it is developed, in the first place. In other words, one cannot have a neutral overview of their coinherence without being already situated on one or the other as starting point of their understanding and relationship as a whole. If this is the case, we can explain why different process thinkers can emphasize one or the other ultimate or try to collapse on into the other, and so on. This is based on the fact that from each ultimate all others integrate differently. From the perspective of God, creativity might be God's prerogative and the world derivative; from the perspective of the world,

God might seem to be only a metaphysical constant and creativity the shadowy essence of ultimate becoming; from the perspective of creativity again, God and the world might seem as instruments of its own aim of creative transformation. I have exploded this "immersion" already in my book *Prozesstheologie* (2000). This is one of the profound reasons for "surrationality" in any philosophically informed multireligious discourse, that is, an inherent pluralism to which I will come back later (Exploration 14).

I will close this section with another important implication of this mutual coinherence, namely, as it is an interesting rendering of the coincidence of opposites—a central notion of apophatic and mystical thought (Exploration 15). In short, as developed by several thinkers throughout different oriental and occidental religious traditions (in fact, in some sense, maybe by most of them)—for instance, Plotinus, Meister Eckhart, Nicolas of Cusa, Ibn 'Arabi, Nagarjuna, and Sankara—ultimate reality is to be understood in non-dual terms. That is, neither is ultimate reality something in exclusion from something else, not anything in exclusion from nothing. Hence, in this ultimate reality, which for many traditions represents divine reality, nothing is differentiated, no opposition is unfolded, and all dynamics are included in the depth of a coincidence of all opposites. Without the necessity, here, to explore the implications of such mystical thinking further, I find this same pattern in Whitehead's antitheses. Although hidden at first, this coincidence of opposites becomes obvious when you ask the question: given the mutuality of God and the world, for instance, in their creativity, or immanence, or unity, what in such an antithesis differentiates God and the world? In fact, nothing! If whatever can be said of God can also be said of the world (as in the six antitheses of Whitehead) then it is the coincidence of opposites that speaks of this non-difference between God and the world. Nevertheless, although God and the world cannot be differentiated by any concept without having undermined the very presupposition of such a differentiation—while we cannot say anything to differentiate God and the world—God and the world also do not fall together or rest in mutual identity. The reason is that the coincidence of opposites is a dynamic coinherence in oscillation. In this sense, the antitheses present us with one of the more hidden, but nevertheless important, places pointing at an inherent basis for an apophatic theology and mysticism in Whitehead (Exploration 15).

Exploration 9

THE CYCLE OF LOVE

MUTUAL COINCIDENCE OF OPPOSITES as mutual coinherence in the oscillation between God and the world signifies nothing less than the life stream cycling through the mutual activity of creative concrescence and transition of God and each event in the world into one another (Exploration 8). Whitehead introduces, reintroduces, the only word left for such a relationship: love. The relational cycle in process between God and the world is best seen through the image of love. It is a symbol, not a concept, because it always already has overflown any conceptuality or logical coordination of concepts, but it has constitutive uses in Whitehead's conceptuality, replacing and turning mere technicalities into lifeblood (Exploration 5).

Although Whitehead uses the word "love" sparsely, he introduces it at important points of the philosophical and religious discourse. At one point, in *Religion in the Making*, he discusses it as the implication of religions becoming aware of the universal coordination of values exhibited by all experiences in their valuation process and by religious experiences in the threefold tension between solitariness, sociability, and universality (Exploration 6). As soon as (rational) religion escapes the tribalism of socialization, it is confronted with a choice between upholding the power structures inherent in the herd psychology of merely social religion (which Whitehead does not consider to exhibit true religiosity) or to counteract them from the experience of mutual relatedness of all things in the value-creating process. It is here that Whitehead differentiates between a "gospel of fear" and a "gospel of love." While the gospel of fear imagines God in the image of the emperor, the tyrant, the war-mongering oppressor and colonizer, the gospel of love pursues the realization of values of goodness, compassion, and coinherence. While under the spell of the gospel of fear one acts because of the fear of God's punishment, the gospel of love inspires the imitation of the goodness of God. This love is the image, the form, the pattern of a universe in which one experiences an aesthetical, that is, valuating, immanence of God in the world process and trusts the aesthetic ordering of the cosmos from its inherent character of goodness. It finds its iconic symbolization by intuiting God as an immanent character of rightness in things, like the character of a friend.

In the last pages of *Process and Reality*, love makes its reappearance again. Here, it becomes the symbol of the two natures of God and their relationship to the world. Since God is all-prehensive in God's consequent nature, God is also all-suffering of the world's actual realizations of values—in their success and failure, their subjective joy and pain, their objective heritance and impact on the world. In light of the Wisdom of God (the valuations of the primordial nature of potentials for any event in light of the highest realization of goodness in their situation), what is prehended in God is evaluated, judged as to its realized and missed potentials of goodness, and integrated into God's infinite, and infinitely good realization of divine relationality. It is cared for with a love that nothing be lost that can be saved. What cannot be saved, the inconvertible evil, is neither forgotten nor emphasized in remembrance, but suffered by God, mourned, and isolated as a mere fact of becoming. The movement of love in the consequent nature is an apotheosis of the world into the kingdom of heavens, not a final resting place of the past, but a living fact in the divine process of connectivity, widening, transformation, and transfiguration into one relational complex of salvation. While beyond concrescence and transition, it remains a living process of becoming in the divine infinity of everlasting life.

Yet, in Whitehead's scheme of creative oscillation, this upward movement into God is not meant to indicate an eschatological end of the world, but turns around into the parousia of novelty for the world. As God is the fellow sufferer who understands, God is also the superject of creativity, that is, the saved body of God *moved back* into the body of the world. Every new moment of becoming is not only confronted with a cloud of (already realized as well as of yet unrealized) possibilities and the pressure of its past to repeat itself in the new event, but with its own reality as it has realized itself not only in the world, but in God's consequent nature. God is not only a mirror of what an event could be—as Whitehead says in *Religion in the Making*—but even more a mirror of what an event could have been in light of divine love so as to be invigorated in its very becoming (which is ongoing) to strive for this realization. In this sense, Whitehead speaks of the oscillating movement of love as the lifeblood cycling through God and the world: suffering the world in love and offering it(self) as new gift for transformation in the world.

In this sense, every living person (becoming as a complex organism with an entirety living nexus) lives in "two worlds": as a process of concrescence and transition in this world, and as an ever-living fact in the presence of God. For Whitehead, this is true not only when realized in religious experiences, but as a cosmological process in every event and all experiences. Not only does God perpetuate God's character of goodness throughout this cycle of love as the character of rightness in all things, but the character of any living person is the creative process by which it becomes a living soul with its life history as the physical body to prove this character. The more it realizes the promptings of goodness in love, the more it will imitate and begin to resemble the entirely living nexus of the Spirit that is God.

In later process discourse, one of the more unsettling issues involved in this movement of love is the question of the status of death and what happens to living persons after death. Can we expect to become immortal? Can we hope for some kind of resurrection? Will our subjectivity survive death? Will we be reborn? Whitehead was undecided on these questions, but not indifferent to their potential solutions—probably not only from personal experiences (the death of his son in the Great War of 1914), but also maybe because of philosophical inclusiveness of his thought given the opposition of religious traditions on this matter. The survival of personality is contentious in interreligious contexts. While for Christianity, for instance, it is of utmost importance, for Buddhism it is a sign of the perpetuation of *samsara*, a state of continued illusion that is, hence, pointless. The same would be true, for instance, for the mutual opposition of different streams of Hinduism: on the one hand, in Advaita Vedanta monism (of Sankara), even the personality of God is an illusion; for theistic leanings (for instance, of the *Bhagavat Gita*), on the other hand, God is the Supreme Person to which we, in truth (as *atman*), relate in love (*bhakti*), not by dissolution. Process thinkers are divided on that matter, too. Some, like Hartshorne, are satisfied with "objective immortality," that is (following Whitehead's terminology), the impact every event has on the world of becoming as a fact of the past. Others, like Marjorie Suchocki and Lewis Ford, find hints in Whitehead's philosophy that allow for a "subjective immortality" (a concept Whitehead does not use), that is, the sustenance of the subjective integrity of the past events not only (through subjective forms) in new events of a personality in the ongoing world, but in their transformation into God's consequent nature.

Without going into particular technicalities, some of the components in Whitehead thought can be collected to gain a better picture. First, in *Adventures of Ideas*, Whitehead admits that it may be true that the relationship of God to living persons (in God's prehension of it) is so intimate, being one of mutual love and indwelling, that this intensity in the cycles of love carries all signs of everlastingness. Second, since the "aim" of the creative process is the integration of intensity and harmony, and since living persons are the utmost expression of the integration of perception (sensibility to its world) and originality (sensibility to divine promptings of unprecedented novelty), it makes sense that "personhood" is the value that God would want to sustain, but cannot if it is bereft of its subjectivity (the entirely living nexus) *as* living. It is in this sense that Whitehead, in his last article, "Immortality" (1941), characterizes God as "personality of all personalities." Third, fitting to this tendency is the fact, discussed just above, that a person lives in both worlds: this one and the kingdom of heavens. Yet, fourth, as Suchocki has demonstrated, the integration within God's consequent nature of the personality not only as a whole, but of all of the events of its life history, into the whole of all other events of all nexuses and societies or organisms indicates a transformation that rather resembles the Buddhist *nirvana* in the total emptiness of self-existence of all events. This also implies, whether as more personal coinherence in the supreme personality of God or as self-emptied diffusion into the whole of the heavens (both in the consequent nature of God), that no kind of immortality, resurrection, or any other eschatological identity, is only a matter of individuality; rather it is a matter of the web of life (within and between both God and the world) as a whole in which personalities are only streams of contiguity or any individual is only a local concentration of infinite fields of relationality (Exploration 2).

In any case, it is one of the often overlooked, but significant, characterizations of the mode of divine "integration" of any event in God's consequent nature that it exhibits at least these two unique features: On the one hand, Whitehead understands this integration not as resting place of the process. Although in God any event would be beyond mundane becoming (either as concrescence and transition), it would unite novelty and memory without loss of perishing. In this sense, however, it would be integrated in God's healing tone (subjective form) of the consequent nature; it would have become everlasting and would remain everlasting in its ongoing integration with God's consequent becoming. In this sense, we can speak (as some process theologians do) of a "resurrection" of the personality as the integrated life history in an ongoing process of divine novelty and in relation to a world ever anew becoming transformed into God. On the other hand, Whitehead characterizes this "state" of an event beyond itself in God as one in which two other elements of becoming are reconciled (as they remain apart in the world process), namely: immortality and immediacy. Not only, then, does any event become objectively immortal in the ongoing world process, being exhausted of its immediacy of becoming and having transcended itself in the process, but its lost immediacy is restored to its history (and beyond to God's universally related prehension of its self). You may decide on your own whether, and in what sense, this indicates immortality of living persons. But what is definite in this scenario is this: that love is stronger than death—yet also that death is part of the cycle of love.

Exploration 10

MUTUAL IMMANENCE

IN WHITEHEAD'S THOUGHT, THE antidote of love appears
as the symbol for the theoretical and practical recognition of the constitution of a universe that in its prehensive
structure is bound together by mutual immanence. In some
sense, all the discussions hitherto have led to this threshold
at which we are able to realize that mutual immanence is
the most ultimate expression of the processual relationality
and relational processuality that characterizes Whitehead's
philosophy, and that its theological implications manifest
process theology in its most profound distinctiveness. It
appeared as the *khora* of becoming and as deepest motif in
the prehensive structure of becoming, in the polarities of
physicality and mentality, of concrescence and transition,
of becoming and perishing, of the coincidence of opposites,
of the coinherence of constricts, in the mutual oscillation
between God's natures and of them with the world in

becoming, of the four ultimates, of the immersion of perspectives, and of the cycle of love.

At this point, I want to further explore two more
fascinating features of mutual immanence: its function as
an intersection of philosophical, religious, and theological
history; and its function as an integration of epistemology
and ontology issuing into a perspective from which we can
gain another glimpse into the mystical side of Whitehead's
cosmology (Exploration 8). It is in *Adventures of Ideas* that
Whitehead paints mutual immanence as inevitable breakthrough of the maybe most profound divine truth (given
its eminent importance, this is not necessarily a hyperbole),
not only in theory, but also as active realization of existence
in the face of God, in the history of "rational" religion, ex-
emplified in the intersection of western philosophy, Plato,
and occidental religion, the Christ event and its theological
interpretations.

It is well known that Whitehead—in *Process and Reality*—had characterized the development of western philosophy (distinct from Indian and Chinese philosophies)
as footnotes to Plato. While experts have debated the exact
meaning of this estimation, at least one thing is clear: it
values Plato's thought and work in its ability to exert such
a power of metaphysical intuition, penetrating vision, and
unprecedented insight that all the philosophical tradition
sin the wake of the event Plato either tries to follow and
elaborate on it, or creatively redirect and improve on it, or
revert and destroy it. The details can be read in any book on
philosophy, not only on the history of philosophy, but in the
labors of current philosophical enterprises. In *Adventures
of Ideas*, Whitehead names as one of the most profound
reasons for this importance of Plato that he *completely*
reformulated the limits in which religious discourse must
develop *if* it has intuited the basic cosmological reality to

be mutual immanence—which Plato, among other things, introduces as *khora* and *receptacle*, as foster mother of the world of becoming, as its the medium of intercommunication (Exploration 3).

The implication of this insight now is that God, which appears in Plato either under the guise of the Good and the Ideas (as they come from the Good) or that of the demiurge—not thought of as an evil force as in later Gnosticism, but rather as the actuality that connects ideas with *khora* in order to activate the world of becoming, somehow as its soul. I cannot go into the details of Plato's triad of ultimate realities here, but it influenced the following millennia in their outlook on the divine (or its denial). The portion that Whitehead takes up now is that of the most profound insight included in this (Platonic) cosmological landscape of the ultimate realities of the world of becoming: that the driving force—whether identified with the demiurge (Whitehead's nontemporal actuality), the Ideas (integrated in Whitehead's primordial nature), the Good (Whitehead's Wisdom, the primordial evaluation of potentials in the primordial nature), or *khora* (either as creativity or as salvific integration in God's consequent nature)—cannot act coercively, but must be essentially persuasive. In other words, God is not a force in the image of Zeus' thunder and the oppressive emperor exhorting absolute power, but in symbolism of the suggestiveness of Ideas (which in Whitehead, differently from Plato, do not self-realize, but are mere potentials judged in the decisions of events), of the seductiveness of the divine actuality (like Aristotle's prime mover not being of causal efficacy, but of the erotic attraction of the *telos*, and in Whitehead's gift of the "initial aim" attracting to the satisfaction of events), and of the capacity to suffer by the prehensive immanence of *khora* (like the all-prehensibility of the universe as a whole, but only always partly in events, and absolutely in God's consequent nature).

The two further steps become the basis for the kind of God's activity regarding the world and its theological interpretation that revealed a deeper understanding of mutual immanence. Whitehead interprets them as the only true metaphysical improvements made on Plato. Although based on a specific religious event, its revelation had the potential—albeit ultimately not the philosophical strength—to realize the dynamic mutuality between (rational) religion and metaphysics that Whitehead had already postulated in *Religion in the Making*: that such unique events contribute in unprecedented and surprising ways to the interpretation of the metaphysical pattern of experiences (Exploration 6). The first step, then, was the Christ event, which Whitehead characterizes as the revelation of God's nature and agency in the world (in the interpretation of Christianity). It revealed God was as love and mutuality—a love that rather suffers than coerces; a love demonstrative not of (abstract) Ideas (as in Plato), but as the actual realization of God's non-violent interaction with the world. The second step consisted in the later trinitarian interpretation of this event as *perichoresis*, of mutual indwelling (of the divine persons in one another, of God in Christ, and of the Spirit in the world). It established, although in highly special form, mutual immanence as the essence of divine being and divine relationship with the world. However, in Whitehead's analysis, neither of these movements has drawn the most radical implications for a universal metaphysical reconsideration: namely, that mutual immanence and noncoerciveness are a profound reversal of Plato's divine reality understood as transcendent immutability (of the Good, the Ideas, and the demiurge), and a reversal of the Christian adaptation of the Platonic transcendence of God into modes of aloof immutability and unilateral omnipotence. In this context, Whitehead's theological view appears as the inner consequence of this unfinished process of the mutual immanence of God and the world without identity and separation in a cycle of love (Exploration 9).

The other face of mutual immanence to be mentioned here appears in Whitehead's late articles and lectures, "Mathematics and the Good" and "Immortality." In this last phase of Whitehead's development of thought, the ultimates of the world process and their mutuality find an interesting turn by which ontology and epistemology become united, and a mystical side of Whitehead's thought—which has already been referred to (Exploration 8)—is revealed. In this last effort to reorganize the ultimates of becoming, Whitehead gives it the form of "two worlds"—the world of creativity and the world of value. While the world of creativity is the process of events in their becoming, the world of value is that of the potentials (so far nothing new). But in a twist of characterization, their mutual immanence becomes obvious when we look more closely at their interrelation and interaction. Then we discover that the actualization of events *is* the realization of values, and that the values are only values in a process of valuation, which *is* the creative process of actualization. Not only is their mutuality unavoidable to understand the happening of the process of a relational world, but their respective ultimates—creativity and God—are now also related in the same way: while the world of creativity can only be creative because of God's primordial valuations of the world of value, God can only be the fact on the ground of the world of value if God is creative.

Not only does this conceptualization exhibit the mutual immanence of the two worlds and their ultimate realities as inevitable, this fourfold (and all of its elements) would, in fact, only represent a mere abstraction if they were not related in such a perichoretic way. What is more, this relationship between both worlds and their ultimates demonstrates the epistemological principle of Whitehead's thought: namely that of a mutual requirement of all categories (although, as will be discussed in Sphere IV, they need not be derived from one another). This mutual requirement postulates that no ultimate element of reality can be expressed if this expression does not use characteristics of the respectively other elements to describe them. Since the world of events cannot be described without recourse to characteristics of the world of value, so neither can God be conceptualized without reference to creativity and vice versa. And none of them (neither God nor creativity) can be named without being involved in the mutuality of the two worlds in the crossing over of categories developed for the respectively other.

Finally, this mutuality gives us another glimpse of Whitehead's mystical side. In saying that both the world of creativity and the world of value are not only mutually descriptive of one another and indwelling in one another, they are also both, taken for themselves, only abstractions from the universe as a whole. Its complex features of unity and multiplicity, God and the world, creativity and value, of the whole of becoming are in the same sense in-different from one another as mutual immanence is immanent in all of their abstract elements and concrete happenings. The two worlds, as well as God and creativity, abide in non-dual unity, but proceed in coinherent movement. While the implications of this processual and relational mysticism will be addressed later (Exploration 15), we might at least note, here, that without this mystical unbecoming of all categories, the process of becoming either falls apart—and cascades into the dualisms it wanted to overcome—or comes to a halt in silence—resorbing all creative existence into mere apophaticism, both of which contradict the spirit of mutual immanence.

SPHERE IV

UNITY IN DIVERSITY

WHILE WHITEHEAD'S EARLIER WRITINGS were mostly focused on aspects of a philosophy of mathematics and physics as well as a philosophy of science from which he consciously excluded the metaphysical and theological questions, they had already developed the groundwork for a philosophy of the event and relationality. Yet, their full interaction (referred to in Sphere III) came to the fore only in the later phase of Whitehead's work, in the lecture series and books delivered while he was teaching at Harvard University, beginning with *Science and the Modern World* and *Religion in the Making* in 1925–1926. It is with these writings (although not exclusively) that, through the reception of his thought by sensitive philosophers, theologians, and social activists, he has historically helped to instigate what became then known as process theology. Thinkers and practitioners of these diverse backgrounds were either interested in a new universal cosmological conception for grounding their visions of social rethinking and change (within and without religious communities) or they approached Whitehead's work from the perspective of social criticism and an early framework of liberation theology—for instance, from the Social Gospel movement—seeking new and broad categories inherent in, or supporting the realization of, their impulse of transformation. These diverse interests probably first met exactly on the occasion of certain events that led to the recognition of Whitehead's work at the University of Chicago in and around 1926. On one occasion, the divinity school invited Henry Nelson Wieman to present the ideas, and elaborate on the theological implications, of Whitehead's work in a lecture before its faculty. On another occasion, the philosophy department (that at the time also entertained the Austrian positivist Rudolf Carnap) awarded a professorship to Charles Hartshorne, who was the former assistant of Whitehead at Harvard and who began to develop his own philosophical theology (or philosophy of religion) on a Whiteheadian basis. And right from the beginning did the coincidence of these events create different modes of reading and interpreting Whitehead's philosophical thought on religion and theology: one more leaning toward experientialism and pragmatism, the other towards the rationalism of the metaphysical tradition. These twin aspects of Whitehead's own methodology—as it sought to integrate the two antagonistic modes of empiricism and rationalism of the occidental philosophical heritage—now became also enshrined in the further development of, and toward, process theology as it began to express a dual gestalt and, henceforth, a long-lasting mutual transgression and oscillation between these leanings. In fact, we can speak of a threefold history of antagonism and mutual transgression borne out from Whitehead's motive (implying a process) of unity in diversity: that between empirical and rational methodologies, that between monist and pluralist inclinations (but always avoiding dualism), and that between philosophical and theological interests.

Because of that essential complexity and universal scope of Whitehead's work (and the contingencies of early reception history), its impact was never divorced from the Christian sphere of thought and influence, nor was it ever confined to it. One needs only to recall that Aldous Huxley's perennial philosophy, seeking a foundation for the unity of religions in global expressions of, and thought patterns revealed by, mystical experience and reflection, could find a companion in Whitehead's *Religion in the Making* as much as the discourse around the relation between science and religion would gain inspiration, new motifs, and conceptual characters in his book *Science and the Modern World*. And while Whitehead in his Gifford Lectures of 1927 on "natural theology," later published as his cosmological magnum opus *Process and Reality* (1929), hinted at the closeness of his work to certain streams of Indian and Chinese thought, so had, for instance, Joseph Needham already confirmed this conjecture in his monumental work on *Science and Civilization in China*. Nevertheless, the first unfolding of process theology happened with the background, and in the context, of western philosophical frameworks as well as the tension between Enlightenment philosophies and Christian theologies (not that Whitehead, in the end, sided with either).

Yet, we must recognize at this point that Whitehead differed in his access from the questions and the prominent battles ensuing from them raised by the philosophical and theological movements up to the turn of the 20th century and beyond in three important ways: he situated his approach neither in the antagonism of metaphysical tradition (for instance, the influential Thomism) versus Enlightenment; neither did he follow Platonism nor nominalism (positivism and materialism); neither did he accept the emerging (and still contentious) opposition between modern philosophy (Descartes, Leibniz, Spinoza, Hume, and Kant) and postmodernity (especially of, and in the wake of, Nietzsche). This means, Whitehead did not begin with a current presupposition (in these three waves of changing paradigms) that in some way or another was shifting the ground toward deism, materialistic monism, and atheism (based on relativism and power analysis), respectively. Nor was Whitehead inclined to defend any of the diverse forms of Christian orthodoxy or to justify any specific development of Christian theology. Although he was widely read in historical and theological (as well as generally religious and interreligious matters), he was disappointed by the failures of (western) Christian theology to pursue a tolerant resonance with multiple modes and ways of religious experiences and their diverse philosophical expressions. In other words, neither did Whitehead set the basis for the religious discourse that would become process theology within the specifics of Christian doctrine, insofar as (and whenever) it would refrain from deeply interacting with metaphysical universality (without giving up its singularity, but becoming pluralistic instead), nor would Whitehead accept for such a discourse any philosophical generality that would dogmatically exclude the reality of the diverse manifestations of religious dimensions of experience as illusions, deceptions, or projections.

Highly critical of extremes of these oppositions as violation of the principle of unity in diversity, or of the uniqueness and universality of experience (in its metaphysical analysis), Whitehead, in a unique turn, developed an alternative mode of thought to the one that seemed to have captured the pivotal point of the whole antagonism in philosophy and theology at the turn to the 20th century:

the "death of God." While bemoaned by many (but still understood as necessary caesura), the "death of God" was forcefully proclaimed by Nietzsche and his philosophical children as *the* inevitable basis for any discussion of religion; and it was later even assimilated into a newly secular theology, death of God theology (before becoming, in the 1960s, a concurrent stream with process theology). Implicitly, Whitehead's circumvention of this "inevitable" basis would also lead to the adoption of Whitehead's strange theological attractor—his new understanding of God not based on the death of God—in an alternative access of process theologies in the late 20th and early 21st centuries to, and fruitful intertwining with, postmodern streams in philosophy (for instance related to Derrida's philosophy of difference and Gilles Deleuze's philosophy of multiplicity) and theology (especially, many forms of feminist, womanist, liberation, and postcolonial provenience) as well as adaptations of poststructuralism. This shift of, and within, process theologies again led, in the Christian context and mediated by Whitehead's own philosophical critique of power structures and methodologies (independent from French postmodern sources, which only came later!), to a similar critique of Christian theology: by developing a theological contrast model born from a deconstruction of the mechanisms of orthodoxy and geared toward constructive alternatives to the prevailing sociopolitical power discourses and practices.

It is no surprise then, given these essential factors of its becoming, that nascent process theology was, from the beginning, between the philosophical and theological fronts, as it faced an equal measure of condescension by, and opposition from, the reigning inherited paradigms in their attempts to stay in power, but also alternative models based on the presupposition of irreconcilable antagonisms that Whitehead tried to overcome. For them (in their poor interpretation of Whitehead's constructive alternative), Whitehead was not going far enough in either battling or accepting the death of God. While philosophers, interested in Whitehead's process approach (including the theological dimension), were put under quarantine because they were still using the G-word (before ironically postmodern philosophy itself opened to theological discourses again at the end of the twentieth century, based on figures such as Derrida and Emanuel Levinas), theologians identifying with similar interests, or even those becoming identified as "process theologians," were from the outset (at least) under suspicion of heterodoxy (if not perceived as being already outside of a tolerable threshold).

Moreover, since philosophers of religion or theologians or religious scholars in the process tradition were scrutinizing the classical metaphysical models, inherent in their own religious traditions and the philosophical patterns they employed from the perspective of their (process) critique of power (especially with regards to its infestations by suppression and violence), they had to expect nothing less than the fierce adversity of those who defended the old conventional models of omnipotence. This scenery played out like a tragic opera in which the ones who feared the loss of the foundation of omnipotence also perceived it as the death of metaphysics per se, and even more (and because of that), as the collapse of the foundations of Christianity itself (or at least Christendom)—paradoxically framing process theology closer to the postmodern streams critical of metaphysical considerations. From a process perspective, however, these traditional categories were no longer anything more than a disguised, seemingly neutral, but in reality imperialist mechanism for the perpetuation of colonization by other (more subtle) means, which (again from a process perspective) had securely to be put to rest for good in the name of a peaceable and free (but more than merely liberated or emancipated) civilization of the future.

Given the concurrent birth of a more pragmatic and a more speculative stream of emergent process thought, back in Chicago, it was to be expected that Whitehead's synthesis of the rational and empirical streams of philosophical thought of the preceding centuries was to be tested soon. What was unified in his "speculative philosophy" and his "metaphysics of experience" became emphasized in process philosophers' and theologians' minds by either the more pragmatist lens of the time and the "radical empiricism" of William James (admittedly an important inspiration for Whitehead) or, conversely, by the rationalist heritage of Spinoza and Leibniz. Some, such as Wieman, were no longer interested in grand metaphysical gestures given the fragility and inherent impermanence of empirical experiences. Others, like Hartshorne, remained committed to a restructuring of the grand metaphysical tradition of the Occident. Since theological interests could be inferred from either of these approaches to philosophy (of religion), these emphases led to the differentiation between (what came to be called) "empirical theology," which disavowed metaphysics (as nothing but a heuristic model for the generation of constants of experience), on the one hand, and "process theology" (in a narrower sense) claiming for itself a new synthesis of metaphysics (in a Whiteheadian sense) and Christian doctrines (although not exclusively), on the other. The former tendency found its way from Chicago to Claremont, California through Bernard Loomer (although only temporarily) and the latter through John B. Cobb Jr. Additionally, this migration to Claremont continued with David Ray Griffin, in his work emphasizing a Whiteheadian philosophy of religion and proving resources to regarding the relation between modernity and postmodernity, issuing in a (holistic) "constructive postmodernism," on the one hand, and a new conversation between science and religion, on the other. In 1973, Cobb and Griffin founded the Center for Process Studies at the Claremont School of Theology (and in affiliation with Claremont Graduate University), facilitating the academic and spiritual unfolding of the latter two streams of process thought (capturing Whitehead's metaphysical innovations for an new kind of theology and philosophy of religion). Therewith, they also created the basis for further transformations of process theology in the midst of, and engaging with, postmodern and post-Christian sensibilities toward ecology and sustainability, feminist theology and postcolonial discourse, poststructuralist and constructionist approaches, as well as multireligious dialogue and non-Christian adaptations of Whiteheadian process categories.

More detailed tracing of the differentiations of these "directions" of process theology and of their mutual differences is at this point less important, because it can be followed up on in great particularity in appropriate and readily available literature (also, for instance, in the first part of my book *God as Poet of the World*). Although, in light of these further developments, we must speak of a multiplicity of process theologies today, to reflect on the motives that have led to ever new differentiations—as process thought moved into different milieus—might be more important in our context since they also reveal the characteristics that still connect them. In all later differentiations, we should not lose sight of the fact that it was precisely the specific mode of unity in this manifold of process discourses—namely, to release multiplicity empowered by a synthesis that demands the production of ever new forms—that embeds process theologies in the character of Whitehead's philosophy itself.

It is nothing less than the inherent creative instability of its principles, categories, and methods, the paradoxical gestalt of which has already been noted, that entails the necessity of an ongoing dis-closure in the production of motifs *structurally* avoiding any closure.

Hence, what must be held responsible for this open-ended processuality is but the underlying dynamic relationship between all of the principles, categories, and methods in Whitehead's work. They can only be understood without grave misinterpretation if we don't take them to mean dogmatic formulations that can be neatly combined to a well-defined doctrine. Rather, we have before us a kind of harmony, not unlike the well-temperate piano, that lives (and dies) by the *mutual immanence* of its elements, which holds them in motion. Such dynamic connectivity means that principles, categories, and methods express their specific "processual unity" only as long as they are neither monistically reduced to one or the other of its elements nor fall apart into arbitrary dualistic isolation or merely pluralistic atomicity. This is their structural demand as Whitehead develops it in the methodological parts of *Process and Reality*, but also in the smaller book *The Function of Reason* (1929), and his last book, *Modes of Thought* (1938): methods, categories, and principles can neither persist in dualistic antagonism nor dissolve into one another. Regarding method, epistemology, and theological content, this mutuality signifies what Whitehead calls their inherent "coherence." It is the (processual) characteristic of this understanding of coherence that (as Whitehead explains) the diverse elements involved are neither derivative from one another nor reducible to one another (the monistic fallacy), although they can never be divorced from one another either without losing their meaning vis-à-vis one another (the dualistic fallacy).

As another corollary, this kind of processual relationship connects form and content, method and categorical analysis, epistemology and cosmology. Coherence becomes effective both in Whitehead's ultimate description of the creative process as mutual immanence of multiplicity and unity, which Whitehead names (the ultimate reality of) "creativity," and in its theological mirror image: the differentiating contrast of God and the world as they are conceived, in their realities, to be related in a process of mutual creativeness. The same processual coherence holds true for the structural instability arising in the description of the process of experience itself, namely, in form of paradoxical coordinations such as that between continuity and novelty, cause-effect relations and creative departures, self-individualizing events and social contexts, the self-perpetuation of characters of "societies" and the vivacity of non-conformal events, as well as the abstract generality of categories and the concrete universality of unique actualities.

As the variations arising from these contrasted elements inscribe in the very dynamics of their mutuality also the unavoidability of a dynamic differentiation of the emphases and weightings of the one or the other, their mutual instability can also help to explain many (if not all) of the actual differences between the divergent models of process theology that have actually developed. In order to further illustrate that coherence and mutual processual immanence can help to account for the reasons for the diversifications between process theologies, I offer three samples: one regarding the variants of the philosophical concept of God; another one regarding diversified appropriations of process theology in the tensions between Christian (Abrahamic) and Buddhist (Dharmic) sensibilities; and a final one regarding the development of an interreligious pluralism.

From its inception, one of the critical points in the constitution of Whitehead's concept of God, which equally aroused enthusiasm and resistance, consisted in the suspicion that, if (as in the case of Heidegger's differentiation between metaphysics and revelation theology) God must not be identified with the ontological ground of the world (generally called "Being," in Whitehead's case "creativity"), God was either threatened to become reduced to a finite being among beings or, at least, would not indicate ultimate reality per se. In either case, the process notion of God would end up signifying something occidental metaphysics and Abrahamic theologies would not recognize as "God." What (historically) added to the irritation of conversation partners of a classical metaphysical background or (assumed) orthodox theological inclination was the *concreteness* of (the event of) God (in Whitehead's sense), which can neither be made to disappear in an abstract principle (as maybe adherence of classical theology to either Aristotle or Plato would have insinuated) nor (in alleged anthropomorphic reduction) exhibit the characteristics of a mundane event or actual entity (let alone of a finite person) among others (as Paul Tillich has taught us to worry about). Yet, rather than being a detraction from the gravity of a metaphysical ground or the concretions of divine action within the world, process theology, by avoiding this alternative, demonstrated a genuinely sympathetic interpretation of (for instance) the biblical dramatizations of divine activity in the world and, at the same time, exposed the unbridgeable hiatus that remained at the heart of the classical metaphysical underpinning of the western theological tradition, namely, that between the ground of being, on the one hand, and the concrete activity of a personal God, on the other.

Indeed, insofar as "God" for Whitehead neither symbolizes an abstract idea nor a mute world principle, but also cannot simply be identified as (or with) a transcendent "person," we come closer to an understanding in which Whitehead's vision and formulation of divine *acting*—being creative of novelty *and* of relations, being infinite *and* with the finite, being of all-embracing universality *and* a healing event—begins to make sense. In and *as* God's reality, God is an *event* that would have to be understood as being sustained by the same creativity as any (world) event, but with the decisive difference that the divine event *first*, by its world-transcendent primordial nature, can become immanent to the world (in every event) without becoming (part of and limited by the) world or becoming lost in it (or dissolve into it), and *second*, by its transcendent consequent nature, can transform the world (events) as they become immanent to itself (Godself) without bursting apart by the world's plurality. For a moment looking forward to the next Sphere on theopoetics, let me restate this divine unity (of reality) in diversity (of natures) as well as the unity of God (as activity and actuality) and the multiplicity of the world (as activity and actuality) in this way: God's activity (creativity) and actuality (the divine event in both of its natures) are *one* (indifferent) in God (as creativity is the activity of and within the actuality of God), but in the world both activity (creativity as ground of being) and activity (self-creativity of any event in both poles) are *differentiated* (distributed among all events and unified as events in the multiplicity of the ongoing process). In God, there is no ontological difference between Being (ground) and beings; in the world, they are differentiated by the ontological difference. But, most importunely, since God is *beyond* the ontological difference, God is neither only one nor only on either side of this difference—neither (the ground of) Being nor one among the beings.

However, many process theologians felt that, besides the technical difficulties of a consistent articulation of this conceptuality, Whitehead's envisioning of God as *one* "grand event" (releasing creativity to all events and embracing them by God's dipolarity of natures) seems not to leave enough space for the *complex concreteness* of events. Singular events (or actualities) in the world are always limited quanta of place and time, are perishing and self-transcending themselves into other events already interwoven within a universal nexus, and are structurally composing "societies" of events with their own characteristics, (actual) worlds, and environments. God as *one* event seems either to miss these characteristics or, at least, to be an exemption to the limitations they impose on the world's actual occasions—and, indeed, Whitehead recognized this difficulty, excluding God as actual *entity* from being subject to the limitations of the impermanence of actual *occasions*. Therefore, different alternative models were developed to accommodate these complex interrelationships of layers of the nexic and societal structures of events, venturing beyond Whitehead's model of God as *one* event, or better: beyond proceeding in the image of the mere *inner* workings of one actual entity. These alternate models, however, were by no means less exceptional in their radicalism with which they undermined the metaphysical adaptations utilized by theological orthodoxies of (some of) the Abrahamic streams while, at the same time, challenging any metaphysical neutralizations of (the possibility of) living experiences of the divine.

Hartshorne, for instance, transformed Whitehead's God "event" into a God "society." Whitehead's God event with its mental and physical poles is meant to signal God's *vivid dynamics* of connectivity with the world from within Godself, that is, with the functions of the primordial and consequent natures. Hartshorne's God society, contrariwise consisting of a multiplicity of God events, is meant to signal God's *consistent character* expressing itself within a plurality of divine world experience (one event at a time) and being collected to one concrete divine society (as a consecutive series of divine receptions of the world). As a divine society, however, the (former) mental pole of God is transformed from a divine process of valuation of potentials (for any world event in which it appears as *eros* of its self-creativity) into an immutable God character, underpinning all God events, in their connected plurality constituting *one* God "person." Hartshorne's vision became known as "neo-classical" theism, because of the fusion of the classical view of divine eternity with divine temporal events and, hence, the combination of divine absoluteness with the absoluteness of divine *relativity* in a new and harmonious way. This conceptualization also manages to highlight the *personal* character of God, which in the process context always needs to be a life history of many events compounded to complex societies of events and nested societies, over the (transpersonal) event character in Whitehead. Hartshorne's insertion also allows combining the immutability of God's personal character (compatible with the classical concept of God) with the living personality of God, that is, the receptive mutability of the concrete society of God events. However, despite this important nod to the classical tradition, Hartshorne's model is only palatable to a theology that would allow for a concrete, immanent complexity of God such as proposed by the more recent "social models" of trinitarian theology (for instance, of Jürgen Moltman).

On the other side of the spectrum of the reception and transformation of Whitehead's proposition regarding divine reality, we find Wieman and Loomer engaged in a process of collapsing one or the other of God's "natures" with creativity (the ground of being) and, hence, tracing out a more pantheistic path. Proponents of this scenario were not only led by a very different theological mood, for which it was more important that God not be misunderstood as a reality among others, but the conviction that God can only remain intelligibly thought to be engaged in the world if God becomes a symbol for the world-immanent creativity of events and world societies, as it resists destruction and combats evil with the ever-creative seduction toward goodness. Some accepted the accusation of pantheism as a badge of honor against predominant religious orthodoxies and as alternative to secular atheism and materialism; others rejected it because it seemed to play into the hands of atheism and materialism. In my own reading of this tradition (which I have developed in my book *Prozesstheologie*), this pantheism is better (and maybe against its initial intuitions) read against the background of the mystical traditions (within theology), which was also an essential (although suspicious) part of the Christian tradition (visible in the likes of Dionysius the Areopagite, John Scotus Erigena, Meister Eckhart, Nicolas of Cusa, Jacob Boehme, and Angelus Silesius). In this reading, the crucial point is not the identification of God with the world as a whole, but rather, like in Plotinus, a oneness that does, at the same time, not identify the whole with its individual parts or moments. Rather, this unity in diversity is about non-duality between the whole and its inherent multiplicity. On this reading, God and world are not identical, but non-different. I will say more about this understanding, which I find fundamental for rendering Whitehead current and process theology fruitful for the future, in the next Sphere on theopoetics.

I will mention four more modulations of Whitehead's concept of God based on the instability of Whitehead's model. They have at least three characteristics in common.

They all shift the relationship between God's natures and creativity in new and innovative ways. Thereby, all of these models follow in their own way the intuition of Whitehead to break with the inherited categories of theological doctrines insofar as they remained bound by imperialist dreams of omnipotence. And they all understand God as an inherent plurisingularity—committed to a thoroughgoing application of the principle of unity in diversity.

One transformation of Whitehead's original concept of the God event can be traced through Marjorie Suchocki, who had also become a substantial force at Claremont. Resistant to Hartshorne's societal view of God (in favor of an event view) and engaged in more contemporary (versus a classical) theological conversations (such as feminist and liberation theologies), Suchocki emphasizes more the personal relationships of a God of love and uses the process view to break with the classical sedimentations that had overshadowed biblical modes of concrete divine interaction with the world to make a difference in engaging with Christian doctrines. Hence, she tends to reabsorb creativity into the divine primordiality. In this sense, she can interpret God as the event and primordial character *of* universal creativity, that is, the event without which creativity would only remain a mere abstraction (and not become the ground of being). In her view, God is to be understood as a community, a divine multiplicity (although not limited to a trinity) engaged in the creative and healing diversification of the world.

Joseph Bracken again differentiates—with reference to Meister Eckhart among others—God as "actuality" (as a concrete, actual happening or entity) from God as "activity" (as the power of creativity itself, which is not itself an entity, but a ground of any event's becoming) without reducing one to the other. In accommodating his Catholic heritage, he widens Hartshorne's God "person" by interpreting the divine "activity" (creativity) as a God "field" (like an energy field) or a "divine matrix" of three "persons" (actualities) *in* which all mundane "actualities" (or societies of actualities) live, move, and have communion.

Lewis Ford, in turn, expands creativity throughput the modes of time interpreting God as the creativity *of* the future that "comes" to every event from and as its future into its immanent present. While by such a movement the divine creativity of the future is pluralized in the present in, and distributed throughout, a world of events, which themselves transform into defined societies as they transition into their own past, God always remains the creative future of the world to (be)come—not an entity of becoming (an actual entity), but always indicating pure becoming.

Another important variation relates to Catherine Keller who understands Whitehead's God (among other symbols) as the act that, in a space of potentialities, breaks the silence of the mere possible with the divine decision to instigate concrete actuality. Facilitating the emergence of creation out of the darkness of chaos, God cuts into, and out of, the infinitely possible the energetic pluralization of finite happenings. Thereby, God continuously brings forth the world as a value process. God sets free becoming as a process in which the divine offer of values in a deep sea of undifferentiated potentials initiate the possibility of a process of self-evaluation of events in the face of an actual world. In a biblical turn, represented by the creation story of Genesis, she reconstitutes divine plurisingularity as the "trinity" of the Deep over the face of which hovers the Spirit of Elohim.

In all of their diversity of interpreting Whitehead's systematically instable coherence, nevertheless, process theologies remain committed to the most profound characteristics of Whitehead's concept of God, namely, that it was meant to facilitate a critique of religious violence and the constructive unfolding of civilizational effects of the categories of relational multiplicity and processual abundance (over and against any reductionism and prematurely stabilized unifications). It is these motives that process theologies brought to bear in their conversations with diverse doctrines when they engaged themselves in a Christian context—not only regarding the doctrine of God and creation theology, but also in relation to anthropology, Christology, soteriology, and eschatology. Again, without necessarily going into any details of these complex, but fascinating, negotiations, we can emphasize a few of the more remarkable characteristics of such process theological investigations into Christian theology.

In some areas, process categories led to genuine re-formulations of Christian teachings. Being divested of the old substance metaphysics and dualistic philosophy, as they were the presuppositions of many of the dogmatic histories, process theologies variously insists that these doctrines can be made in new ways to release what they wanted to say in the first place, but what had been blocked by the old categories. I will just name some of these motifs: a new emphasis on the inviolable mutuality of transcendence and immanence of the divine reality in relation to the world process, even a universal "incarnation" of God in every event; a new intelligibility of the emphatic relationship of God with the world in all of its events and societies, even in the form of God's suffering of each and every event in its interwovenness with the cosmos (God as "fellow sufferer who understands"); a new understanding of divine all-presence in all world events, although with the eschatological twist of God's future continuously creating time for the self-creative becoming of the world; a new access to the impermanence of becoming as a perpetual renewal of creation in every moment of its existence (*creatio continua*); a reinvigoration and reformulation of a Johannine Logos-Christology in connection with contemporary Wisdom- and Spirit-Christologies; a new and surprising way of comprehending the classical doctrine of the two natures of Christ and their communication of idioms; a new interpretation of the social character of (original) sin as a demonic reality of the repetition of the destructive past in the constitution and becoming of new events (as this situatedness undermines and a priori limits potential freedom); a new access (actually, several) to the question of the theodicy emphasizing the non-violent relationship of God to the powers of the world; a contemporary restatement of the realities of a new heaven (consequent nature) and a new earth (a new cosmic epoch); and, last but not least, an imaginative reformulation of the reality of immortality (although in a thoroughgoing relational way) as a form of the ingathering of one's life history to eschatological identity.

In other areas, we find that process theology's inherent "critique of religion" (*Religionskritik*) led to quite unorthodox illuminations of classical Christian doctrines insofar as they seem to contradict the impulse of essential relationality in the articulation of God language. Here are some of these more outrageous motifs: that the world is not created out of nothing, but is, in fact, eternal (although not in its current gestalt); that God must in some way be understood as multiplicity, but not necessarily as trinity; that there can exist infinitely many worlds and, hence, that this world (this cosmic epoch) will not be destroyed in an apocalyptic act of God, although this Earth may be obliterated through human activity, will not exist eternally, and will in this vast universe sometime in the far future sink into oblivion; that the human "soul" does not possess natural immortality, but rather only an existence beyond itself, and that we can only hope to be gathered to an eschatological unity in the memory of God; that God intends, and has the power to effectuate, the universal salvation of the passed world and that the "kingdom of heaven" is *now*, in the consequent nature of God, present to this (and any) world; and, to add one more, that the self of human beings is in its self-identity continuously becoming, is embodied in a "society" or "community" of events of experience, which are intricately related, and can find self-identity only in a divine act of transformation that ultimately transcends it own power of integration.

Although these motifs might be out of sync with Christian orthodoxies, interestingly, these same motifs blend exceptionally well with, for instance, Buddhist thought: that all the events constituting the world in its very becoming are impermanent; that each of them in its internal process of becoming is a "suffering" of its inherited past out of which it begins to constitute itself as a process of the integration of its relations beyond itself hinting to karmic entanglement (*samsara*); that events (actual entities) are momentary formed happenings like *dharmas*; that the world is one relational connex of *dharmas* in the process of co-origination (*pratitya-samutpada*); that God in God's "natures" is like the Buddha nature (in its cosmic universality as *dharmakaya*) all-receptive, all-compassionate, allwise, and all-knowing; that the consequent nature has the "form" of *nirvana*, namely, the "form" of (and beyond) a formlessness, abiding in and beyond the diffusion of all in all; that this (divine) "all in all" does neither know of brokenness nor death, but is bliss; that the world has neither beginning nor end (God does not create, but saves); that God spans infinite worlds like the *Lotus Sutra* claims with regard to the infinite multiplicity of Buddha fields.

147

The fact that we can find similar resonances with other eastern philosophical and religious traditions—such as diverse thought patterns of Hindu, Jain, or Daoist provenience—has led to a variety of interreligious dialogues using the means of process theology. Following Whitehead's intuition in *Religion in the Making* that the two contemporary "catholic" (in intent and conceptual potentials universal) religions might be Christianity and Buddhism, it is not a surprise that one of the most outstanding and long lasting of these conversations happened at Claremont between John Cobb and Masao Abe (representing Zen Buddhism and the Kyoto school of Buddhist philosophy). The same resonances have furthered studies utilizing process approaches in contributing to (and transforming) current discussions around religious pluralism. Some of these pluralistic models draw in various ways on Whitehead's coinhering ultimate realities (God, world, and creativity) in order to comprehend the diversities of religious forms of experience and existence (forms of life). These pluralistic process approaches have the advantage to be able to intelligently elucidate the genuine coexistence of such traditions not contrary to, but as expressions of "absolute" truth. Yet, they also allow for new theoretical foundations for the understanding of new forms of "hybrid spiritual identities"— something I have called "transreligious" processes. Other models build on the plurisingularity of each and every actual reality, which realizes its deepest character by manifesting the complex "nature" of God. From this perspective, it becomes less self-evident that God would become manifest in only *one* event generating just *one* religion as ultimately true (commonly identified with the Christ event). Such a reading, again, would be most compatible with the rhythm of prophets and imams in Islam, of the recurring avatars of Krishna in Vaishnavism, of the repeating arising of the

Buddhas in both Theravada and Mahayana sources, and of the infinite cycle of divine Manifestations in the Baha'i Faith.

The pluralistic variants of process theologies have also been connected to, and differed from, other forms of religious pluralism, for instance, the pluralistic thesis of John Hick (another former Claremont professor). Hick's pluralistic thesis rests on a Kantian epistemological presupposition: the differentiation between phenomenal and noumenal reality (that which appears and that which something is in itself, respectively). While this differentiation allows Hick to address the relativism of any phenomenal religion to be based on the unknowability of the noumenal reality of the divine, it exhibits the weakness of basing its negative theology on the Kantian isolation between the mental apprehension of physical reality and the unknowability of this reality in itself. Contrarily, the process understanding of experience (as prehension) does not remain bound by this separation of patterns of cognition of the sphere of mind, on the one hand, and the allegedly unknowable reality of objects of cognition of the empirical world, on the other. Since the experiential (prehensive) process consists in the mutual processual immanence of all realities, it indicates a transformation in which from objects of experience (which are themselves already units of experience) new subjects of experiences arise, which themselves again transcend themselves as objects of new experiences. On this view, the character of a process approach to religious pluralism is markedly different. It is not the inviolable apophatic unknowability of ultimate reality that would function as the foundation of a pluralism of religious truths, but it is the essentially incomplete process of experience in which the ever-new constitution of relations in new revelation events harbors their relativity of truth and furthers their plurality of appearance.

This process pluralism is also congruous with Whitehead's understanding of divine reality—especially as developed in *Process and Reality* and *Adventures of Ideas*—as the unity of which reveals itself in the divine ability (through the primordial nature) to release infinite potential worlds into actuality and (through the consequent nature) to harbor infinite actual realizations of worlds in harmonious form. God's "aim" (subjective aim) with the world is not pre-determined (has no ego), but is oriented toward ever-new realizations of harmony and intensity within, and of, worlds. In the musical image of "harmony of harmonies," Whitehead presents God as aesthetic (that is, feeling, becoming, transforming, creative, and healing) actuality/activity (effectuating actualities from potentialities) without which no world would be really possible (could become actual); in the immanence of which the world remains open in/as/to processes of relational plurality; and without the transcendence of which the unity in diversity of the/any world would fall apart.

Exploration 11

TRANSPANTHEISM

It has become common to characterize Whitehead's understanding of the relationship of God to the world in terms of the concept of "panentheism." Hartshorne brought it back into the discussion in the 1940s—and from there it flourished again as a general theological term to designate *the* alternative to classical theism of the surviving mind-set of the Middle Ages, on the one hand, and to the deism of the Enlightenment turn to scientific foundations, on the other. While classical theism insisted on the unilateral power of God and the transcendent attributes of omnipotence and immutability, deism tried to save not the sovereignty of God over the world, but God from disappearing from the plane of existence in light of the independence of the world in light of its causal material closedness propagated by the emerging scientific materialism. In any case, the presupposition was—as Whitehead reminds us—an unchecked substantialism and its implied dualism. Substantialism not only insinuates "independence" as the highest value so that relationality and change must be derivatives, secondary derivations, and basically irrelevant additions, because a substance needs nothing for its existence except itself. But substantialism also lives from an inherent split between the dominating substance and its dominated attributes (and its accidents). Paradoxically, not even such a dualistic substantialism can exhibit some kind of coherence if it does not already, but in an unacknowledged hiddenness, presuppose relationality, and be it just in the necessary dialectic of master and slave—something Hegel and Nietzsche would exploit. While classical theism saw the independent substance of God dominating the accidents of a contingent world that is in change, deism was the last resort of the profound shift to the dominance of the world of which God now seems to have become an accident that, in further consequence, could be discarded altogether. This again was made possible by turning Plato's domination of the Ideas over matter around into the domination of matter of which mind and spirit became, at first, disposable accidents and later, inconceivable illusions.

Contrary to this eternal war of dominology, Whitehead's recovery of mutual immanence as the most intriguing implication of a relational cosmology of the world process most certainly escapes the flaws of dualism (Exploration 10). His event cosmology with its (over the course of Whitehead's work) shifting multiplicity of related ultimates of, and in, process arrived at a wholly different beginning, namely, from the prehensive constitution of experience as the most basic ground for exploring the constituents of the world, the understanding of our mental constrictions being part of this process, and a whole new notion of divine reality in relation to such an inextricable mutuality of insistence. Whitehead's most powerful instruments—visible in the layers of dualities in oscillation in all realities and the reciprocal presupposition of its related categories of under-standing—are precisely these: to revert dominologies into univocally diffused fields of reciprocity. I will name only two of the conceptual shifts employed.

One is the shift from Plato's Ideas as real realities to events as real realities. As long as (Platonic) forms could be understood not only as ordering patterns, but also as high-est actualizations of themselves, the realities of the world were only shadows establishing their domination, in fact, something that should not be at all (*me on*), and actually "is not" (*ouk on*) since their becoming is their unreality. Here, form (actuality) dominates matter (possibility). This of course changes with the nominalism of the late Middle Ages and the reversals of the Enlightenment era. For, then, forms become shadows and universals are mere abstrac-tions, so that matter dominates form as it has in itself all the activity. What did not change, however, was the substantial-ist dominology of one over the other. It was not the least relativity theory and quantum physics that changed this understanding of matter again radically. Not only became time, space, matter, and energy exchangeable, or better: mutually transmutable, terms, but the dialectic of particle and wave, of location and field, and of the reality of po-tentials in the quantum realm with the locality of particles (after the breakdown of the wave function) demonstrated the flaws of the classical presuppositions as defect and ir-reconcilable with the new science venturing from, and breaking through, them. This was exactly the point White-head was making in *Science and the Modern World*: that the metaphysical presuppositions of Enlightenment science (its scientific materialism) was self-defeated by the sciences it produced, and that it needed a new metaphysics that expresses these new findings (rather to contradict them) and makes there realities understandable. In Whitehead's reciprocal view, then, Plato's forms have mutated into mere possibilities *for* actualizations (they are not actual or even actualizing for themselves), and matter is just another abstraction from self-creative actualizations of events, namely, the real potential for the ongoing process of actualization in new events, nexuses, and societies. In fact, their separation has become inadequate, a mere abstraction from the concrete process, and their difference, even in their inherent polarity in form of mental and physical prehensions, is one of reciprocity and oscillation.

The other shift is as consequential for the new understanding of the relationship between God and the world—and whether it should (and in what sense) be subsumed under the term "panentheism"—as is the first. It concerns the substantialist mold for conceptualizing ultimate reality. While for classical theism as well as for deism (and the ensuing atheism) the "ground of Being," the metaphysical ultimate, falls in one with the most real reality, which for that function must be most sovereign and independent, Whitehead de-substantializes ultimacy. Now, it could neither be identical with God nor with any replacement substance, like matter. This is one of the reasons (the other will be discussed in Exploration 12) for Whitehead to not equate, like classical theism, God with ultimate reality—or the metaphysical with the religious ultimate—but, instead, to differentiate God from creativity (as one of the most persistent names for Whitehead's metaphysical ultimate). Nor is the metaphysical ultimate now identical with matter, either in the Aristotelian sense or in the Enlightenment sense. While Aristotle's matter is passive potential, Whitehead's creativity is the activity of actualities (events); and while Enlightenment matter (in classical modern Newtonian physics) is inertia in movement only of its arrangement, Whitehead's creativity is prehensive, experiential, mental, and physical, in its occasions, but for itself, a mere abstraction from the process.

In a certain sense, Whitehead's differentiation between metaphysical and religious ultimate—although more complicated than that (Exploration 10)—resembles Heidegger's differentiation of *Sein* (or Being or the ground of Being or the Being of beings) from God, but also differs in two important regards: first, the "beings" that really "are" in Heidegger's sense are really only human beings, the only beings that experience Being, while this experiential structure is true for all events in Whitehead; second, and most importantly, Heidegger's Being was not only hostile to the religious occupation of ultimacy in the form of the notion of God, but reabsorbed the divine attributes back into Being. In the later work of Heidegger, being mutated from the activity that arises in the consciousness of beings as their ground, but is actual only in them, to the self-revelation of Being in the history of certain beings—the philosophical races of the Greeks and the Germans. This had devastating implications, as Heidegger became the prophet of the self-historization of Being in the superiority of the German race and his support of Nazism. What that outcome demonstrates is only the danger that comes with the reabsorption of agency into metaphysical ultimacy.

Whitehead, instead, came to the conclusion of the differentiation between God (as transcendent actuality: actual, but nontemporal) and creativity (as immanent activity: non-actual, but temporal)—but also, not to forget, their mutuality in creativity's transcendence of any specific event and God's immanence in every event's initial aim. Thereby, he first circumvented any dualism, but second, avoided any remaining substantialism in the ensuing alternatives of monism and pluralism—as exhibited by the remaining substantialism of Spinoza and Leibniz. Against Spinoza, Whitehead insisted that the monism of *Deus sive natura*, the identification God and nature, remained within the dominology of substantialism, because not only was the infinite actuality identified with the infinite activity exhibited in the multiplicity of nature, but the multiplicity of natural beings (modes) had no real existence besides being shadows of divine attributes, which they are identical with the divine substance of nature. Contrarily, when *natura* is de-substantialized (of God or divine substance, activity, and actuality), then, *Deus* cannot be its ultimate reality, but immanent creativity is. And if God cannot remain identical with creativity, creative events arise out of their shadow existence into that of self-creative actual beings in the world of becoming. While this move away from Spinoza had already historically led to Leibniz's pluralism of actual existents, Whitehead still saw a remaining substantialism in Leibniz insofar as God in Leibniz's monadology remained the dominating unity of all monads, the monad of all monads, which again reserves the perceptivity of all reality for God alone. While Spinoza's modes of being were mere shadows of the divine substance, Leibniz's monads stayed closed to the word, that is, although they are related through God, they remain isolated substances in the world of becoming. Whitehead's solution was that of prehensive self-creative occasions, immanently exhibiting the ultimacy of creativity, but being mutually related to divine reality, which is also self-creative and, not being a substance anymore, now symbolizes the event of processual relationality par excellence.

In order to evaluate the label of "panentheism" for Whitehead, we need to take into account two additional facts. On the one hand, it is clear that Whitehead neither followed classical theism nor deism, neither monism nor pluralism (in its substantialized form). To use panentheism for his position instead seems to make sense since it proposes that God is not a transcendent dominator, but that the world is *in* God (in some profound sense). Not only is God immanent in the world (as many version of classical theism, for instance, that of Thomas Aquinas or Moses Maimonides, would also affirm)—and as Whitehead's does with the primordial nature. Rather, with panentheism, it is Whitehead fundamental conviction that God suffers the world, understands it from the inside, and inhales the world as fully prehended into God's consequent nature, which in divine healing is the apotheosis of the world *into* God and its everlasting life *in* God. It is this reciprocity of mutual impact, or better, mutual prehensive coinherence, that binds Whitehead's God to panentheism.

On the other hand, Whitehead's uneasy relationship between metaphysical and religious ultimates—as they in their reciprocity remain in a conceptual movement of not only oscillation, but becoming and renewal (what I have called "immersion" in Exploration 8)—explains how many process thinkers could develop different perspectives and emphases from the orientation toward classical theism (with the neoclassical agenda) or, on the far other end of the spectrum, pantheism (with a naturalist agenda). In this process pluralism, panentheism seems to be a conciliatory solution that can embrace many of the diversified motives of the whole field. It exhibits a strong enough integrity to remain identifiable in discussions with other forms of theism, deism, monism, dualism, and pluralism; and it offers maybe the best chance for its religious availability. Additionally, in my own interpretation, it allows for the realization of common patters with several stream of mystical and apophatic expression of religious experience such as can be found in Plotinus, Sufism, and Vedanta. So far, so good!

My hesitation to subscribe without reservation to the use of the term panentheism for Whitehead's position is based on my understanding of the radical nature (the de-substantialization) of the ultimate of ultimates in White-head's thought: the mutual immanence—ontologically and epistemologically—of God and the world (as the over-arching contrast representing all other contrasts). Let me explain this thought with three perspectives. First, panen-theism grants only asymmetric reciprocity. God always remains the exceeding "more than all" (God is in all, but exceeds the all of the world) to which creation conforms as the embedded "less than all" (the world, per definition, can-not exceed God). But Whitehead, instead, understands mu-tual immanence as mutual transcendence: both God and the world exceed one another and, only for that reason, can be seen by Whitehead to be mutual instruments of novelty for one another. Hence, Whitehead's panentheism is rather one of mutual *transcendence*. Second, the cycle of love (Ex-ploration 9) between God and the world knows of no all-embracing unification of the multiplicity of the becoming of, in, and between God and the world that would not be pulsating back into a new multiplicity. Hence, Whitehead's panentheism is one of mutual *trans-unification*. Third, as long as the asymmetrical embrace of God has the last word, the duality of God and the world is still haunted by a sub-stantialism of reservation and superiority. Hence, as I have elaborated in my book *The Divine Manifold* (chapter 13), instead of the label of panentheism for Whitehead's posi-tion, it would be much more adequate to characterize it as *transpantheism*: as oscillation of mutual transcendence, mutual trans-unification, and mutual non-identity. White-head's movement from of de-substantialization—to which panentheism must be subjected, too—has led him through a non-substantial pantheism (in which neither God nor the world can claim final unity for themselves) to a non-dual (non-different) transpantheism beyond unity and multiplicity in mutual in-sistence. The pulsation of mutual immanence reveals a transpantheistic creative pleroma of God and the world.

Exploration 12

INSTEAD OF A THEODICY

THERE IS NO SUCH thing as a theodicy. Well, this may be an exaggeration. Maybe I should reformulate: no worked out theodicy has ever satisfied so as to let the profound question it raises become smaller (than the question). In the play *Danton's Death*, Georg Büchner declares it the rock of atheism on which all claims of the existence of God must shatter. While the problem is old, it was formulated by Leibniz as the question of how we can justify the existence of God in the face of the inexplicable suffering not only inflicted by humanity upon itself, but also by living beings upon themselves, by nature upon humanity and living beings, and maybe by the very fact of the existence of something rather than nothing upon all existents. Buddhism, insofar as it knows of no creator God, variously attributes it to the ignorance of desire and self-possessiveness or the materialization of spontaneously arising dreamscapes within the *dharmakaya* to reiterated illusions that claim self-existence.

Christianity attributes it variously to the sin of humanity against the law of God or, in a cosmic context, the hubris of angles.

Of course, the presupposition for Leibniz's question is a classical theism for which God must be at once omnipotent and absolutely good. The existence of evil either demonstrates that, if there is a God, either God is not omnipotent, because God would exclude evil and suffering, or not good, affirming evil and suffering in some way. Various answers were based on the manipulation of the concepts involved: how to define power, goodness, evil, suffering, divinity, cosmos, and so on. But this manipulation of the content of one concept leads always to shifting meanings of all others, making a defense of classical theism unlikely, but, at the same time, producing other forms of religious ultimates, related to the world as in revisioned forms of theism, pantheism, monism, naturalism, atheism, deism, or panentheism. In the end, the question does not go away as long as we experience evil and suffering beyond the boundaries that we impose on the concepts invented to understand them.

Leibniz himself answered his question in a fragile, but still instructional, way—namely, through the interaction of the relational boundaries of all involved notions. If we want to live in a world of relationality and freedom, it needs to have the potential of grades of goodness, which includes the mutual limitation of its features, which again either appears as, or includes, or does not exclude, or demands, evil and suffering. The forms that evil and suffering take, however, are contingent in the infinite possibilities of how the ingredients come together as a whole. The best possible world is the one in which they reach the highest harmony of mutual limitation. For Leibniz, this is our world and, hence, God must be its creator by expressing in it the best harmony between power and goodness. Whitehead, on the other hand, does not know of a preestablished harmony in the mutual limitation of the involved terms since he does not limit the potential infinity of actual worlds to one world in which harmony equals stabilization. This would be a balanced relational world, but it would not know of process, becoming, oscillation, the movements of life, and the cycles of love.

Process theologians have taken at least two routes to answer Leibniz's question. One answer, which comes from the rational, theistic branch, has focused on the boundaries of power. Griffin rightly refers to Whitehead's permanent imbalance of becoming, which never reaches any final realization of harmony and, hence, can only always strive for new realizations of harmony and intensity. He also correctly concludes that in a world of relationality that does not exclude God's being from being relational must redefine the creative power of God. Insofar as creativity is not reserved for God, but rather distributed among, and in, all becoming as the very condition for its existence (the metaphysical ultimate as immanent self-creativity), neither does God cause, nor, therefore, can God be responsible for that which the whole body of events, nexuses, and societies co-creates, with or despite God's suggestions and seductions to the best possible vision and realization in any moment. While classical theists criticize this attempt to establish a theodicy by eliminating one of the most cherished divine characteristics, the omnipotence of God, from the perspective of a criticism of power in the image of the absolutist dominator (as in contemporary postmodern theologies), this is rather its strength: love must be relational, no matter what.

The other answer comes from the empiricist, pantheist side. Bernard Loomer does not compromise the power of God, that is, understand the existence of evil based on any lack of divine power, but rather focuses on the boundaries of goodness. For Loomer, God is not an event, but the whole of the creative process, the mystery of the web of existence as such, its womb of possibilities and creativity. God's power is one of goodness insofar as God can withstand the clashes mutual limitations of happenings impose in such an all-connectedness of the universe. While all existents always operate from their limited perspective, their goodness is always limited and evil is unavoidable. But the mystery of existence is that despite these limitations, the world does not fall apart, that it is a whole that can resist the disintegrating movements within itself. This mystery is named God, because it signifies the "stature" and "size" of divine power to integrate evil within the body of the good, or to actualize goodness despite the evil this body produces. The power of God is the bearing of the whole not to dissipate despite its "integration" of good and evil. While there is no lack of power in this design, now the purity of goodness seems to be compromised. But then, we need not forget that many monistic and apophatic religious traditions have walked a similar way—such as the historical Kabbalah, some braches of Sufism, and Vedantic monism as well as certain tantric branches of Buddhism—by not excluding evil from God or ultimate reality.

Instead of following these theodicies further and instead of finding a theodicy in Whitehead, I want to follow Leibniz's intuition to understand Whitehead's recourse to questions of evil and suffering from his emphasis on the mutual immanence of the ultimates of the relational process *that is* the transpantheistic pleroma of God and the world. Since harmony and intensity are the highest aims of all processual movements in Whitehead's universe, the mutual *limitations* of the ingredients involved will reveal their relevance for the question of evil and suffering without becoming a stabilized equation of that which in a universe pervaded by events of experience can only be lived, but not be solved. I will follow a track of four such delimitations: the mutual limitation of God and creativity; the mutual limitation of infinity and the finite; the mutual limitation of goodness and power; and, finally, the mutual limitation of process and reality.

The mutual limitation of God and creativity has two reasons. One was mention in the last section (Exploration 11), namely, that their collapse would reinstate, or not over-come, the substantialization of the metaphysical ultimate. Yet, I have, thereby, also hinted toward the other reason: the devastating implications of such an identification, as it implies a dominology and justification of oppression, or the transfer of divine attributes to the metaphysical ultimate, as it risks the superiorism of particular histories (of race, gen-der, color, ethnicity, class, or religion). Indeed, in *Science and the Modern World,* Whitehead introduces the notion of God *only* because he found a way to escape both impli-cations, and he does so in the same context: with a non-substantialist interpretation of creativity in difference from the religious ultimate, which then again can only appear in a multiplicity of experiences and conceptualizations, al-ways escaping monarchianist domination of one particular interpretation over another. With this "principle of empiri-cism" (Exploration 15), God must, at the same time, also be a "principle of limitation"—not the ultimate limitation (the ultimate as limitation), but the *actual* limitation of the ultimate (creativity) in a process of universal co-limitation of self-creative events, nexuses, and societies constituting one or another universe. In this sense, it is precisely the awareness of the question that the theodicy poses that is at the ground of the differentiation and mutual limitation of God and creativity.

The mutual limitation of infinity and the finite is essential to the understanding of Whitehead's process universe. Infinities abound—the infinity of potentials (eternal objects), the infinity of spontaneity and freedom (creativity), the infinity of relationality (*khora*). They are nothing but that: abstractions *from* the actual process. Only the event of experience itself (and its interconnections) is concrete, actual, driving the process. But the event is finite: it is the concrescence of the infinities, their interaction, their growing together to *something* rather than, remaining mere infinity, nothing; and it is the transition of this concrete something, a fact, issuing into new processes. Hence, Whitehead attributes the creation of value, of something of worth, of importance, something that makes a difference, to events, the processes of valuation. Only events, in their finiteness, can be of value; infinities are (in and of themselves) worthless. Nor can God only be conceptualized as infinity, then, but must be understood as the initial concrescence of these infinities. While God's natures are infinite in their expansiveness and range, they are processes of valuation, infusing, incarnating, and receiving finite processes of value. Whitehead criticism of Spinoza and Leibniz, therefore, is not only that they somehow retained the infinite substance of God, making finite processes irrelevant or isolated, but also that God must be the connecting event in which infinities and finiteness interact and coinhere. The goodness of the process cannot be abstract either, it must be happening in the infinite multiplicity of finite value processes, which again will produce mutually incompatible values, grades of importance, and tensions between the potentials worth striving for (and attainable) and the ones actually reached. Evil is an implication of this pleroma of value processes insofar as a final balance of harmony and intensity is unattainable.

The mutual limitation of goodness and power is an implication of the multiplicity of value processes. Whitehead is, with Augustine, of the opinion that there is no positive evil as such, but only a privation of goodness or value. This means on a most basic level that nothing that becomes can be of zero value since all becoming is a process of experiential valuation and its vectorial perpetuation beyond itself. Any becoming is the actualization of a good. But the goodness of events is contextual: it is limited by its actual world it is to be born into; by the real potentials of its past (its heritage); by the available cloud of possibilities yet unrealized, but applicable to the situation of the event; and by the inherent power of the valuation process to take decisions, more or less being able to preserve its past without exclusion and to transcend itself in the realization of its potentials. Then again, events are part of nexuses, societies, organisms, and layers of environment in which their own goodness can be mutually reinforcing, but also hindering, their development. Every good may be limited by its scope of the situation in which it arises and the scope of the future that it effects. But there will always be inconsistencies with environments, organisms, societies, nexuses, and events in their concurrent alternative realization of values. What is good in a smaller horizon (say, my life) may be devastating for the wider horizon (say, the history of a society). Hence, the power of goodness is limited by the prehensive sensibility and the power of vision into the ever-vaster background of the cosmos, the depth of the past, the fainter horizons of environment, and the far removed future. Finally, although God's goodness incorporates all sensibilities of omniscience and is, therefore, not limited by the self-creativeness of world events, its power of realization is. On a deeper level, however, one may say—as Whitehead does in *Religion in the Making*—that God's power is limited by God's goodness: that all valuation of God are always good to the utmost; that the measures by which God evaluates are that of love, compassion (co-suffering), and justice (evaluation and co-ordination of all actualizations); and that God never wishes for the actualization of potentials of evil worlds. But as the good needs never violence to prevail, God's goodness is limited by its inherent power of non-coercion. And since God's power is suggestive and prehensive, it is always one of suffering of the world not suggested, but incorporated. There cannot be either any process of valuation or any realization of goodness (as well as of evil) that would not be a process of suffering. God, in Whitehead's words, is, therefore, "the fellow-sufferer, who understands." And God's saving power is born from this form of prehensiveness.

The mutual limitation of process and reality means, in this context, that nothing can either be only in process or a factual reality. The implication is fascinating, especially in light of several contemporary undertakings—for instance, of John Leslie and Keith Ward—to understand the world as a product of God's mind, existing only in God's mind (Exploration 3). We remember that in Whitehead's view the world of creativity and the world of value are mutually immanent such that both are mere abstractions from their coinherence (Exploration 10). We also remember that in view of a transpantheism as more adequate description of Whitehead's understanding of the relationship between God and the world, both God and the world are not only mutually immanent to one another, but also mutually transcend one another (Exploration 11). This means, here, that their processes are never absorbed by one another and their reality is a fact beyond their internal process. It is this self-transcendence in the oscillation of concrescence and transition that virtually demands that the world is not only a dream of God's inherent process of valuation of potentials, but a reality beyond Godself, a self-transcendence of God's concrescence into a transcendent creativity. This is the reason that Whitehead, at one point in *Process and Reality*, adds a third "nature" to the two divine natures, namely the superjective nature: God's self-transcendence. If, then, the world is real on its own terms and pursues its own processes, maybe (as I have argued in my book *God as Poet of the World*) this accounts not only for the difficulties process theology has with concepts of creation out of nothing, but also the true place from which to start any theodicy: that love is real only in mutual self-transcendence and that the reality of the world with its suffering and evil is an unavoidable fact of this process.

Exploration 13

RELIGION AND PEACE

LOYAL RUE, IN HIS naturalist account of religions, defines the reason and meaning of the existence of religion (in an evolutionary universe) as humanity's striving for the well-being and wholeness of the individual and of society. One could understand peace to be an expression of this aim and its reality. Yet, religion and peace are by no means identical or necessarily mutually supportive. Whitehead is not blind to the factual evidence of religions throughout history being, if not the instigator of wars, cruelties, oppression, and inhumanities of all kinds and sorts, so at least the fertile ground for all sorts of opposites of peace. Peace, on the other hand, needs not to be connected with religion, but can be a necessity of survival in certain situations, as it might be the contingent outcome of convergences of events that for themselves have not had this intention at all. And then there is also the necessary differentiation between the embodiments of both religion and peace: religion is not an idea, but a real complex social phenomenon; peace is not an idea either, but often the hard won absence of war and (certain degrees of) violence, always only under local and temporal restrictions. Realizations of one's humanity and religious teaching, respectively, can be the spiritual roots for projecting images of religious *and* peaceful ideals that develop a power on their own, but they are never identical with their real incorporations or failures to incarnate in worldly states and processes.

In Whitehead's analysis, both the reality of religion and the reality of peace inherently relate to the same metaphysical situation of a universe in processual connectivity in the multiplicity of its realizations. It is the reality of the *aesthetic* character of existence. As all concrete happening and all of its compositions into organisms and environments are based on the prehensive structure of experience, they are aesthetic in a twofold sense: First (regarding the receptiveness of physical and mental poles), experience is the perception of otherness into concrescence. This is the original meaning of *aesthesis*: perceptiveness. As we have seen, for Whitehead this is not limited to sense perceptions, but is the fundamental expression of existence to be the becoming of something in an inherent and surrounding field of fellow creatures (Exploration 5). But second, since any process of concrescence is a process of the valuation of these prehensive insistences, it is also an aesthetic process in the sense of the creation of new integrated realities of harmony and intensity or artistic processes evoking beauty. In this process the artist, then, becomes the artifact, transcending itself back into a "cosmos" as an aesthetic community of coordinated beauty.

God's immanence in this process is, for Whitehead, precisely that of such aesthetic oscillation between perception and beauty. In fact, in Whitehead's own estimate, this beauty is the only self-justification of existence, and all events in their mutual immanence contribute to it. So it makes sense when Whitehead goes on to call the reality of God in relation to the world the "harmony of harmonies." As this aim of God is always the realization of ever new harmonies and intensities, and as love is the expression of how God wants to bring this about, beauty becomes one of the main Whiteheadian constituents of the non-coercive realization of societies in the universe—a process that he calls the civilizing process of the cosmos—besides truth, art, adventures, and peace.

With these sister terms of beauty, we also approximate Whitehead's notion of peace. I will relate it to religion later. As in *truth* we cannot circumvent the recognition of otherness in the prehensive process, and as *art* and *adventures* are essential moments of a process that does not decline to mere repetition of nature or the "naturalized" (realities we artificially create, but perceive as natural, like our prejudices), *beauty* has the same relation to *peace* as has *evil* to *tragedy*. What does that mean? It means that the vast causal influences that constitute the past and environment of any becoming organism make it hard to not get caught up in the habit of mere repetition of the past, even if its is one of violence and oppression, but that the turmoil of alternative, competing, and incompatible forces of this past (and environment) forces new events to either succumb to or to develop into new and different harmonizations without the loss of intensity inherent in its complex past and environment. The creativeness of the event is its artistic solution of this conundrum: harmonization and intensification. What is more, no artistic escape is permanent, as it must be re-evaluated in ever-new adventures of its permutation in new events, organisms, and environments. Hence, the beauty of this aesthetic process is *not* peaceful per se. It can be cruel, evil, and demonic. But if we may with Whitehead assume the whole unending process to be pervaded by divine aesthetic of a harmony of harmonies, deeply engrained in the aesthetic processes and their turmoil, then we have already assumed not only that the world process is always being lured into an *ideal* of peace that can forgo or transcend the aesthetic havoc for embodied coinherence, but that this hope is already *based* on the reality of divine concrescence (and the release of the universe) being the all-pervading, coinherent reality of the (primordial and consequent) Spirit of peace.

Peace, in Whitehead's words, is the remembrance and overcoming of tragedy. Tragedy is the unredeemed reality of the aesthetic process in which beauty has become evil, because it missed the aesthetic harmonization without loss of intensity, but instead pursued over-harmonization, which is always suppressive, or over-intensification, which indicates possessiveness of individual integration without care for the impact on the environment. Peace is the integration that can let go of such a past as self-repetitive evil, but remembers it as its heritage. In God's consequent nature, peace is the reality of an apotheosis of the world into the kingdom of heaven as the healing remembrance and transformation into universal wellbeing that Loyal Rue is talking about. But what about *this* world? It would seem that the consciousness, embodiment, and realization of *this* peace is the reality of religion, the spiritual reality by which religion can claim to exhort wellbeing, healing, and wholeness—or be worthless.

The spiritual reality of religion is, in the human realm, that which can be expected if God is the harmony of harmonies. But why, then, are religions historically often, even if they claim the opposite, the ground of hate, oppression, inhumanity, war, and violence? For two reasons:

First, although the reality of God's consequent nature is immanent to this world through God's superjective self-transcendence by which God rejuvenates the cycle of love, and although God lures toward the realization of the Wisdom of God's primordial valuations for any event; in other words: although God is incarnated in the world as *eros* and *telos* of peace—the aesthetic impulse plays in any society, secular or religious, its own game of self-creative insistence on itself. This equals the degeneration into substantialism, atomism, and the clash of forces, as motifs for the emergence of the fatal feeling of dogmatic superiority: one religion must win the contest (hostile exclusivism)! Second, although religions are the awareness of the reality of divine peace, the havoc caused by aesthetic limitations tends to identify the parochial aesthetic insights and practices as identical with divine aesthetics, divine evaluations, and divine harmonies. This equals a relationalism without process, issuing in the fatal feeling of mystical superiority: I can wait! In the end, you will come through the eye of my truth (imperialistic inclusivism)! Both of these errors, that of dogmatic insistence (with its blind superiority complex) and of mystical self-identification with the divine (with its eschatological supersessionism) are the production of evil (evil in the making) and its resulting tragedy is the absence of peace. The prehensive and experiential nature of the recognition of deep divine harmonies has degenerated into the possession of truth, the suppression of adventure, and the oppression of art, in favor of evil self-perpetuation of one's parochial pit.

What follows are some Whiteheadian circumscriptions of the nature and function of religion and peace. Religion is the coordination of the tension between solitude, social embodiment, and universal openness of the aesthetic process of valuation. Religion is the coordination of the process of valuation of the individual, the community, and the relevance of them with the universe as a whole. Religion is the recognition, surrender to, and realization of, the importance and value of all processes beyond themselves. Without religion, Whitehead says, the world would just be a mass of suffering lighted up in a meaningless conglomeration of suffering events. Religion is a vision that seeks the eternal in the perishing world without the loss of novelty. Religion is the consciousness of the mutual immanence of all processes and realities in the faint consciousness of a character of rightness inherent in the world of becoming that is the harmony of harmonies waiting to be realized in a civilizing process of society.

Peace is the innermost reality of religion as it symbolizes the divine aesthetic of intensive harmony in the midst of the adventure of becoming and the havoc of self-indulgent beauty. Peace is the overcoming of self-centeredness; it is self-transcendence to the widest horizon of the harmony of harmonies without ever becoming self-identical with it. Peace is the loss of self and personality insofar as they are inhibitions for the aesthetic recognition of universal mutual immanence. Peace is not an ideal of which we lack realization, but the motive force of the Spirit to presupposed under the turmoil of the body of the universe, organisms, societies, and environments in their pursuit of limited aims, waiting to be discovered and embodied. Peace is not a product of efforts, but it is the gift already given with the very existence as aesthetic reality and its realization of self-transcendence. Sure, Whitehead's peace is not the absence of war; it is not the contractual negotiation of conflicting self-interests; and it is not the possession of any religion or society or spirituality, for that matter. But so is religion not a possession, but the embodiment of the power of peace, the incarnation of its reality, and the pursuit of its promises.

Peace, in Whitehead's sense, can be experienced in the midst of the adventure of becoming without being spiritualized. In fact, it is at the very initiation of any event the *eros* of its becoming. Yet, it is unattainable as a possession. It cannot be attributed to the individual, but only becomes real in the reciprocal embodiments of societies, organisms, and environments.

As religion has arisen through the excess energy of creative freedom, freed from the necessities of life, the rehearsal of sacred myths and the intensification of feelings, combined with the intellectual penetration of the realties of the universe (Exploration 6), so must peace be the recognition of the mutual immanence of all of these necessities and excesses of freedom, realizing their harmonization in the mutual intensification of the rhythms of self-creativity and self-transcendence.

Peace is the ultimate reality of mutual immanence (Exploration 10), and the spiritual realities of religions are the aesthetic breakthrough of that ultimate reality *in the midst* of this process, waiting for, urging for, luring toward its ever-new embodiment, but always endangered by the confusing of our experiences of it with the illusion of self-insistence in, and the sin of self-identification with, it that has haunted the history of religions.

While, in Whitehead's view, religion is (with science) the force of civilizing humanity, it can only do so if it exercises peace as the inhibited perception of the forces of oppression, exclusion, and the stigmatizations of minorities and the marginalized. Peace is the suffering of the recognition of this exclusion and the suffering of the consequences in standing up against them in its own non-violent mode that will be religious insofar as (and to the extent that) this sensibility reflects the harmony of mutual immanence as divine witness against the forces of destruction.

Peace is already *there*, when we begin to search for it. Peace is God consciousness: the realization of the ultimate reality in the midst the illusion of separateness and the demonic power of exclusion—not dissimilar to the universal Buddha nature we all share (*dharmakaya*) while ignorant of it, or the realization that *atman* is *brahman* (*tat twam asi*). Religions are the scaffoldings in which to embody this God realization in light of, and in resistance against, illusion and demonic perpetuation of exclusions and oppressions. There can only be *many* because of the exclusion of exclusion.

Peace is the *immanence* of the entire living nexus of God, the Spirit, in the nexic body of organisms and environments and universes. Religions are the structured societies that, if and to the extent that they succeed in breaking through the dark clouds of illusions and evil, harbor, expand, realize, and yearn for *its* life (the life of *that* Spirit), which is everlasting in the midst of becoming.

SPHERE V

THEOPOETICS

WITH THIS LAST PART, I want to introduce my own synthesis of process theology. Although some of the emphases of the landscape of process theology discussed up to this point were mine, in my own work over the last decades, insofar as it was concerned with the research, development, and application of process principles, categories, and conceptions, in many ways nothing has more determined my own understanding of the irreducible character of process theology than the growing conviction that process theology is before all else "theopoetics." This last Sphere will be dedicated to a sketch of some of its perspectives.

The expression "theopoetics" has its own history and an expansive field of cognate meanings. In the 1960s, a theological school under this designation flourished on the east coast, which was in its turn influenced by Whitehead. In the works of Stanley Hopper, David Leroy Miller, and Amos Wilder, it figures as an alternative to the conceptual systematics of classical theology and the literalist hermeneutics in the use of religious language and symbols. However, while Whitehead did not abandon efforts toward "system" (although of an open, always unfinished, and paradoxical system of relational processes), these thinkers highlighted the essential poetic nature of religious language, which divulges its mystery precisely where it disrupts all categories of grasping. In another form, Catherine Keller—teaching at the same university as this theopoetic school, namely, Drew University in New Jersey—has taken up the term, now in tandem with "theopolitics" and a critique of imperialist patterns of thought. In a completely different context, "theopoetics" first appears in antiquity as the elongated form for *theosis*, the oriental Christian symbol attempting to point at the aim of creation (and human existence) to be, and to be reached in, a process of "deification": theo-*poiesis* as *becoming* (being made, being re-made in the image of the) divine. And even in this meaning, the term "theopoetics" is close to Whitehead's articulation of the ascension into, and transformation in, the consequent nature of all events: the "apotheosis" of the world into God, which crowns the last pages of *Process and Reality*. In the European context again, the term "theopoetics" may appear to have signaled a mode of thought contrary to the *Theodramatic* of Hans Urs von Balthasar. Yet, this impression is deceiving, because Whitehead's use of "poetics" hints at Aristotle's *Poetics*, which was less oriented toward the verses of poets than the drama of tragedy as the highest art form. Whitehead understands the world process as a dramatic effort of a dynamics of peace that urges (without coercion) always the creative transformation of the variously occurring antagonisms into contrasts. The "tragic beauty" of this poetic process does not denounce the tragic manifestations of this drama, but in their remembrance limits their effect on the process as a whole.

In general, Whitehead's use of "poetics" corresponds to his *aesthetic* mode of thought for which language as such is only one form of symbolic interaction, while expressing the experiential structure of all existence and indicating the creative essence of reality: that any actual reality cannot be grasped in its facticity alone (which was Whitehead's basic argument against scientific materialism), but is as it happens a process of decision and, hence, valuation, and, therefore, always creative of values. Events are *aesthetic* processes: they become as valuations, that is, as actual decisions among potentialities, and they are, when they have become, realized values. Moreover, it is precisely the aesthetic presence of God in the world through which the world is intricately intertwined, as community of relational mutual feeling, in a process of the creation of value. Value creation *is* world creation. And it is the same dynamics that releases the impulse of civilizational development toward the aim of a peaceful society of the future, and which would all the more be able to mirror the relational nexus of the world in its profound aesthetic nature. In this sense, "theopoetics" is—in Whitehead's phrase—a sign of the dramatic nature *of the adventure of the universe as one.* This oneness is not a variant of the oppressive power of forced unifications (as deconstructive critique must uphold against dogmatisms), but the *aesthetic* process of the manifold of value creations that Whitehead's has offered us to meditate on with the radical contrastive antithesis *that God creates the world as the world creates God.*

Despite all of these resonant variants in Whitehead's work and beyond, my own use of the expression "theopoetics" has aimed at the unfolding of a specific passage in Whitehead's final part of *Process and Reality*, which is committed to the exploration of God-world dynamics. In this passage, Whitehead signifies God as the Poet of the world and supplies the meaning of this designation with the following connotations:

> The universe includes a threefold creative act comprised of (i) the one infinite conceptual realization, (ii) the multiple solidarity of free physical realizations in the temporal world, (iii) the ultimate unity of the multiplicity of actual fact with the primordial conceptual fact. If we conceive the first term and the last term in their unity over against the intermediate multiple freedom of physical realizations in the temporal world, we conceive of the patience of God, tenderly saving the turmoil of the intermediate world by the completion of his own nature. The sheer force of things lies in the intermediate physical process: this is the energy of physical production. God's role is not the combat of productive force with productive force, of destructive force with destructive force; it lies in the patient operation of the overpowering rationality of his conceptual harmonization. He does not create the world, he saves it; or, more accurately, he is the poet of the world, with tender patience leading it by his vision of truth, beauty, and goodness. (346)

Whitehead describes a threefold creative process, being that of a world in turmoil, but in its complex embodiments being embraced by the infinite potential of the divine primordial nature and the transformative receptivity of the divine consequent nature in which the whole process can find to its healing unity. Of the many connotations in this text that could be explored from this threefold structure of the creative process, I will only highlight three that characterize God as Poet: God is not the creator of the world, but the healer of the world process; God participates in the world not in the form of power or might, as cause among causes (or as its most mighty cause), or cause of causes, but in form of the gift of meaningful realizations and of the transformative gathering of broken actualizations; God acts in non-violent patience and seducing tenderness with the aim of achieving (ever more intense) harmonies. Theopoetics is the unfolding of an understanding of process theology that is committed to *these* elements. It is again not possible, nor necessary, to follow all implicated lines of thought; yet, a few final remarks will suffice to round out the main points of interest.

The most important insight of theopoetics (in my current meaning) can be found in the confirmation that Whitehead does *not* identify divine reality with the metaphysical ultimacy of creativity. With this insight, another profound decision is reiterated—as it has made it possible for Whitehead to introduce the concept of God (in *Science and the Modern World*) into his philosophy, in the first place: Only if God may *not* in the classical metaphysical sense be understood as omnipotent creator (*ex nihilo*) does it become possible to withstand the devastating effects of the question of theodicy. The reason is that the classical concept of the all-efficacy of God (the first cause *pantocrator*) would posit God in such a competition with the effective causality of any world event, society, or entity—which is directly excluded by the theopoetic passage—that would not be able to generate any reasonable excuse for the character of suffering in which the world finds itself seemingly inextricably immersed. Not that God cannot act "in power" or "mighty" is of importance here, but that the *understanding* of divine power cannot be defined by invoking causal efficacy anymore. The divine act, we remember (and as any act of an actual entity in becoming) is not modeled after the push and pull of physical causes, or more philosophically, from setting something outside of itself (as a transeunt act), but from a primordial *receptivity* and the gathering of itself out of relations to other relational processes. Whitehead introduces for this alternative to acting as coercion, which is not how God acts, the term "persuasion." It wants to capture God's tender seduction to meaningful and intense harmonies of peace in the midst of the wreckage of the world as the cosmic process is caught in the antagonisms of power struggles. From this estimation (and in the same context), Whitehead also draws the interesting consequence that divine activity, since it does not act in causal identity with itself (and, hence, cannot be identified as effective cause), but through the initiation of always unique creaturely creativity, can never be recognized or known without concrete experiences of "revelatory events" in the multiplicity of their symbolic presentations and creative adaptations in concrete landscapes (societies and characters, histories and cultures). God must always anew be named in novel events of self-disclosure.

The poetics of the redemption of the lost and of the healing of the broken contains a spiritual and ethical impulse to personal and structural empathy countering unnecessary suffering. Yet, it also urges to take an active stance contrary to the production and repetition (prolongation) of structures of suffering (or, conversely, their mitigation, prevention, and overcoming through the remediation of the causes and media of social and political upheavals and wars) insofar as they are sustained and propagated by a misguided religious consciousness, clerical striving for power, and parochial orthodoxies. Indicating a process of unification in diversification, this persuasion would maybe best understood as a process of education that—not dissimilar to the ancient (theological) notion of *paideia*—could facilitate a decisive step toward an engaged embrace of a multiplicity of practices of truth in, between, and beyond religions.

In a deeper sense, it will only be through such a "divine poetic" that a new (and already in all religions present and as present accepted) dynamics of "identity" can be effectively enacted—the poetic identity of an expanded consciousness of the universal interwovenness of our little lives as individuals and communities with the world process as a whole in its ecological connectivity, demanded by Whitehead's ultimate category of mutual immanence. If theopoetics sheds light on these rhythms of oscillation between all realities and their ever-unfinished harmonizations in a world of becoming and perishing, it does so not on occasion of existential angst, but for our acceptance of the impermanence of our identities. Theopoetics demands a mystical spirituality of the unification with the world of the Poet in the flow of divine (persuasive) activity through it. Without dissolving into the Poet, rather holding the world in this oscillating flow, we are called to hope for our unification with the poetic process *in* the interwovenness of the manifold that is the world and to feel it in every new event of its happening.

Although the Poet does not dissolve in this mystical process either, the Poet is immanent to it with "absolute" transcendence. The Poet does not collapse with the world *precisely because* divine reality always remains in a unique way *apophatically subtracted* from it, that is, it can never be grasped by the categories of the world. Neither can God be positioned *in* the world nor *beyond* it; but in apophatic manner, God is always *equally and at the same time* (but absolutely inadequately signified in this way) "absolutely" transcendent and immanent. In resonance with both mystical and cosmological thinkers like Meister Eckhart and Nicolas of Cusa—and maybe strikingly even more so with

Plotinus—I like to speak of the "in/difference" of the Poet presupposed in (and, as Derrida would say, "older than") any language that remains trapped in the dialectic of immanence and transcendence, identity and difference, unity and plurality. This Poet's in/different, "absolute" difference from the world consists precisely in holding the world "*in* difference" as it *affirms* its multiplicity. In other words (as I have already developed from my early exploration of Whitehead and mysticism on two decades ago): the Poet of the world does not "exist," but *in-sists*, that is, insists *on* the world of relational multiplicity in process and, at the same time (and therefore), insists *in*—is *more inherent, internal, and immanent* to—this world process than it is to itself. This God *in* (the in-sistence in and on) the manifold is the Poet *of* the manifold—*the divine (in) multiplicity—its* unfolding (the *explicatio* of the primordial nature) and enfolding (the *complicatio* of the consequent nature). In this relational manifold, the Poet becomes its healing immanence insofar as this healing becomes manifest in the ecological translucency of *mutual* being towards and within the other. Here, the resonance of theopoetics with the *theosis* of which eastern Christianity speaks so deeply is illuminated in a new way: such a theopoetics induces *ecotheosis*.

These explorations into theopoetics have already been developed in light of poststructuralist sensibilities, especially with regard to the axis between Whitehead and Gilles Deleuze—the French philosopher of multiplicity and inheritor of Whitehead's emphasis on creativity and novelty as ultimate expressions of reality. In this context, the poetics of mutual immanence can also open a pathway to a democratization of the categories with which we labor to understand the world in and around us and as a whole. Instead of the monopolistic and imperialistic hierarchies of causes and principles of classical metaphysics as they have become effective in classical philosophical and religious doctrines of God (and still are influential), Deleuze points toward the *univocity*, the "one voice," with which all creation in its unique multiplicity speaks of its relational existence (*ex-sistence* here meaning with Richard of St. Victor: to exist from, or out of, one another). Hence, understanding this democratization as implication of the poetics of mutual immanence (this book has made effort of convey) helps us to grasp one of its most radical implications: that of the *groundlessness* of the world. Because of the process of rhythmic creative oscillation between God and the world, which is indicated by this conceptuality, we can dispossess ourselves of the necessity to seek security and foundation in any ultimate reality of substantialist nature. Instead of lingering within the realms of ultimate realities (such as God, world, and creativity) and ultimate relations (between those ultimate realities or between divine persons, for that matter), the mutual oscillation itself does not create the necessity for naming any foundation—beyond the oscillation itself. Ultimate reality, then, in a theopoetic view, is not a "reality" (a *relatum relationis* or *relatio ipsum*), but the groundless processual relationality of ultimate realities *itself*. The medium, the middle itself (the fragile, not the extreme), is ultimate; all is *intermezzo* in all else.

While theopoetic in this sense was already the leading idea of my book *God as Poet of the World* (2003, 2004)—and especially of the programmatic 2008 *Postscript* to its English edition—it found its current form in my book *The Divine Manifold* (2014). In it I have also drawn out its maybe most clear formulation that cycles back to the first point made: the difference between creativity and divine poetic. The multiplicity of elements named to characterize theopoetics (in this context) are best understood if we avoid the language of creaturely creativity with its collages, collections, and collisions of powers and forces *completely* for the signification of the Poet and, instead, speak of a divine love that is precisely defined in such a way that it cannot in any way be expressed in the language games of powers and forces without already having sold the Poet to these powers and forces in an act of idolatry. The love of the Poet, which for Whitehead circulates between God and the world, is in this sense not a power, neither all-power (omnipotence) nor any comparable force, but a reality sui generis: this love *in-sists* as *polyphilia*. As "love in/of/as the manifold" she embraces and co-inheres the All in the mode of *in/difference*. *This* love is "absolutely" different from the powers, which she makes possible, suffers, and transfigures beyond their capacities. In the mutual sympathy of all with all, she begins to manifest her redeeming and healing continence. In this *ecotheosis*, she commands her in-sistence in the multiplicity; but she initiates it ever anew as its medium. She *subtracts* herself from mundane "identity" as *affirmation* (subtractive affirmation) of the community of becoming. In this "absolute" in-sistence and polyphilic in/difference of apophatic love, the world becomes her poetic body.

Exploration 14

THEOPHANY (INSISTENCE AND POLYPHILIA)

THEOPOETICS, IN THE MEANING applied here, can be understood as an extension of the relevance mutual immanence plays in Whitehead's work—as was discussed throughout the book. Both exhibit the same three characteristics in the relationship between God and the world: their mutual incoherence without identity; their mutual transcendence without isolation; their mutual resonance or oscillation without ever abandoning processuality. The first characteristic allows God to be the Poet of the world, meaning: the world is "made" God in the sense of a *theosis* (*apotheosis, ecotheosis*) in the consequent nature of God and—in the cycle of love—offered in this transformation back to the poetics ("making") of the world. The second characteristic highlights the *poiesis* ("making") of God by the world, meaning: that the self-creative reflection of the divine in the world process creates poetic images of God—diversified in every event, nexus, society, organism, and universe, all religions are expressions of this poetic creativity that is not identical with God, who remains the mystery of all of them. The third characteristic assures that there is no definite state of satisfaction to either the process of God creating or of God being created; nor is the implied becoming of God through our self-creative reflections ever identical with God's self-creative becoming in God's natures.

Nevertheless, this divine poetics is, as the quote from Whitehead has shown (Sphere V), not identical with the creative process either—be it that of the self-creative "making" of the divine images or that of divine transformation of the world into, and in, God's consequent nature. Rather, this divine poetic is the "making" of the self-creative process one of healing, wholeness, and salvation. As, in Whitehead's thought, God is not identical with creativity, God's poetics is not creativity, but the gift of transformation of creativity through the mystery of God into peace, that is, a movement of mutual immanence presupposed in, and underlying, all creative processes (Exploration 12). It is the immanence of the harmony of harmonies in the creative process of the worlds; the unprecedented, unexpected, ever-new intensification of its satisfaction (perfection) in which an event either feels the "perfect moment" or is transformed into the everlastingness of life without loss. Religiosity and religions (at their best) are the "salvation" of this feeling in the nexuses and societies of becoming: the feeling of the eternal within the ongoing processes of the becoming of worlds and the organizations of processes to societies that know of this peace as their ground and aim.

Theopoetics, in this sense, indicates the being of God as the love that cares that nothing be lost (if it can be saved), and as the care for the ever newly to be realized peace at the ground or in the midst of the process of the becoming of all worlds. In this sense, Whitehead affirms in *Process and Reality* that an event can in the midst of its (nexus of) becoming feel perfection as a momentary glimpse of the presence of eternity in becoming. Even in the fragile reality of perishing events, the Poet may appear—Whitehead says unashamedly with Plato—as a moving image of eternity. It may become a theophany of peace: the shining through, the translucency of the realms of becoming and divine salvation. (I will come back to this presently.) And because of this feeling, whatever its rationalization and whatever image is used to express it, in this theophany an event may feel the promise of peace of mutual immanence in the divine saving in Godself (the kingdom of heaven) and in the ongoing process.

In *God as Poet of the World*, I have named that which becomes realized (recognized and activated) in this theophanic event the "theopoetic difference": not the difference between Being and beings, creativity and self-creative events, not the ontological difference, but the difference between God and creativity, which is now the difference between love and power. While power always remains an expression of creativity, love is the essence of divine poetics. It is because of this theopoetic difference that what I name a theophanic event, Whitehead describes as the realization of fearless love, as it, for instance, becomes translucent in the Christ event, or as universal compassion in the Buddha event: it reveals the nature of God and how God acts, namely, without force, in prehensive suffering and in poetic saving; or it lets the mutual immanence "appear" as ultimate reality of wisdom (of self-emptiness) and compassion.

In *The Divine Manifold*, however, it has become central to understand this love—beyond any conception of power—as not being divorced from the creative forces of

becoming, but to present itself as their "subtractive affirmation." The theopoetic difference does not establish a new
dualism of good and evil, of light and darkness, but names
the movement of the *diffusion* of God in the multiplicity of
becoming, of the love *of* the multiplicity of becoming. This
infusion of the divine *in* multiplicity names the *in-sistence*
of God; and the divine love of multiplicity identifies this
in-sistence as *polyphilia*.

I have introduced the term "insistence" already (Exploration 1), namely, as the prehensive internality of an
event in itself in the process of concrescence (in-sistence *in*)
and as the self-transcendent superjectivity of an event into
other events in the process of transition (insistence *on*). It is
another way to name mutual immanence as processual and
oscillating reality of realities. If we accept God to be understood as an event (although a unique one), this could be said
also of God: that God in-sists *in* Godself by the insistence of
all events *on* God to be valued by God (the consequent nature), and that God in-sists in all events (primordial nature)
by being insisting *on* all events (superjective nature). Yet
here, the term has a more pronounced theophanic meaning: God does not "exist," but insists, in-sists *in* the world
by diffusion in all processes, and insists *on* this *in*-sistence
through polyphilia, the poetic love of multiplicity.

This is the movement of God's poetics: God is the subtractive affirmation of multiplicity that in the *affirmation* of
the multiplicity of the becoming of events, nexuses, societies, and worlds subtracts itself from its creative process as
its poetic, theophanic peace. Neither is it identical with the
self-creative process nor is it different from it (Exploration
15). Rather, it is beyond any identity and difference, as they
are always defined from the framework of the world and
its symbolizations of the divine. It is not the power of love,
but the love *in* all power, saving its havoc of becoming from

eternal loss and indulgent intensity that lacks harmony. It is theophany: the translucency of divine harmonization *within* the adventurous becoming, its instigation, and its everlasting meaning. It subtracts itself *from* all identity with all becoming by, at the same time, in-sisting *in* becoming as the affirmation of becoming, as multiplicity.

It is in this context that I understand the curious fact that Whitehead never attempts to prove the existence of God. At various places, he even criticizes these attempts as irrelevant. And being aware of Hume's criticism in his *Dialogues*, in *Process and Reality*, instead of functionalizing God as a metaphysical principle, he takes recourse to the experience of the "Galilean vision," of the love that by patience and gentleness operates throughout nature, and that becomes even more theophanic in the unique experiences of religious figures such as Christ or the Buddha. That God does not exist, as a being, as an identity, or in difference from the world has been already established in the analysis of the six antitheses of *Process and Reality* (Exploration 8): there is no characteristic in the mutuality of God and the world that can be reserved for reasons of differentiation and formulating the identity of God counter to the world; but neither does this inability imply the identity of God and the world. This is what divine subtractive affirmation means: the diffusion of God in the world, in-sisting in it *beyond* both identity with it and difference from it. The God who does not exist, in-sists as polyphilic insistence *on* the process to become in its multiplicity of worlds, and in-sisting *in* this multiplicity as its poetic love that cares.

Divine in-sistence and polyphilia condition one another. They indicate the divine peace as theophanic translucent experience. However, they also insist on the recognition of the failure to manifest this peace. In light of its experience, not in spite of it or by the absence, this theophany insists on the recognition of and non-violent, non-coercive, persuasive stance against the imperialistic unifications that undermine, make invisible, erase, and destroy the multiplicity of becoming. Polyphilia recognizes the marginalized, the excluded, the minimized, the last, the least, and the forgotten. It exhorts the spiritual and ethical intuition, impulse, and experience, of the value of all becoming in its full complexity, divergence, and multiplicity. It sides with a religiosity of remembrance, of the tragedy of suppression and exclusion, and it arises within a praxis of religion that counteracts these oppressive unifications under the imperialistic, patriarchal, racist, sexist, misogynist, classist One. It strives against dogmatic monopolism and a Manichaean division of humanity. It predicates a multiplicity of poetic expressions of religions, a plurality of religions, because they are understood as theophanic experiences of, and ways in, the in-sistence of God and the mutual immanence of their inexhaustible and indispensable plurality. It functions as foundation for a meaningful religious pluralism: a polyphilic pluralism (Exploration 15).

Finally, on a cosmic level, the theophanic in-sistence of God will also insist on the mutual translucency of all organisms and environments in a cosmos. It is not true that the world consists of mutually isolated levels of being, of hierarchies of organisms and structures. This was the idea of "the great chain of being" between the (despicable) matter and God, the pure spirit. But there is no gnostic flight from the world. Polyphilic in-sistence is rather that *of* all levels of evolutionary organization of a cosmos with all others. It is a *cutting through* all hierarchies of power and self-subsistence, of substantialist exeptionalism and justifications of hierarchical authority. Every event has, besides its embededness in different layers of evolutionally complexity of becoming also to some extent *direct* access to all other levels. It is (only) through this directness that all events, be they of matter or spirit, particles or persons, *feel* the world and feel a *world*. Feeling does not need consciousness, although its intensity will be enriched by it. Nevertheless, the in-sistence of God also means such a divine diffusion in the world process that divine theophany of love *and* the mutual poetics of love cannot be differentiated from one another, but are related by subtractive affirmation of one another. All happening is bound together in an *ecotheosis* of the theophanic manifestation of peace (Exploration 16). It is the illusion of the opposite that haunted eastern religion, and it is the demonic perpetuation of the opposition to it that horrified the western religions.

Exploration 15

MYSTICISM AND PLURALISM

DIVERSE INSTANTIATIONS OF PROCESS theology have always not only had a leaning towards religious pluralism, but also actively contributed to its important questions: Can there be more than one true religion? Can various religions be genuine ways of divine theophany and salvation? Can such a relativity of religions be justified against claims of exclusivism and inclusivism? If we can discard the parochialism of the exclusivist position that only one religion can save or be true or be ultimately superior to others, but also avoid the hidden violence of the inclusivist position (seemingly more soothing to the dogmatic minds) that ultimately one religion (my religion, of course) has ever been more true so as to be, in the end, revealed as the only way (poor unconscious others!), what would a pluralist position look like, coming from the process universe of discourse?

I will not discuss the many suggestions offered from other universes of discourse, here, but will directly address some of the pluralistic patterns of response to these questions and some of the answers process theologies have attempted. I will, then, relate my own suggestion of polyphilic pluralism, as developed in *The Divine Manifold* (Intermezzo 2). It can be pointed out ahead that mysticism and apophatic theology plays some, and at times an important, role in all of these endeavors.

In general, the main answers have gravitated toward three solutions. First, exclusivists and inclusivists can, but by no means must, be *pragmatic* pluralists (leaving it to the mystery of God to decide) insofar as they appeal to either the grace of God to handle all nonconformists resisting (or being unaware of) one's own, but ultimate, truth with mercy whenever the truth will be revealed to them (after death or publicly at the end of the world), or as they defer the consequences for outsides (to that truth) to the wrath of God, which is not our business (the wrath is mine!), and understand its imperative (in the meantime) as divine request for tolerance. The more inclusivist the view (since there is a gradual scale between exclusivism and inclusivism), the more will the former motif (grace) replace the latter (wrath). On the far side of inclusivism, such as that of Karl Rahner, not only the individual salvation of non-believers (or other-believers), but even the independent existence of different religious communities is to be understood as part of God's plan. On the verge of a theoretical pluralism, such inclusivism will see the symbolisms at least of the "great" of the world's religions as positive vehicles of the ultimate reality of one's own religion—much like Raymond Panikkar's Christ in Hindu symbolizations of Krishna. But then, certain streams of Hinduism, Buddhism, and Jainism will claim the same in reverse: that Christ is an *avatara* of the

Great Divine Person known as Krishna; that whatever illusion you believe in, the realization of the Buddha nature in all living beings will finally free you from *samsara*; and that whatever truth you believe is true, the final realization of the truth as mediated by the omniscient *tirthankara* will hit you sooner or later in one of your millions of lives to come.

While this first solution identifies one's dogmatic positivity with the metaphysical ultimate, the second solution insists on the irrelevance of any universal ultimate, at least in the sense that it cannot be expressed, in principle. The reason for this abstinence of expressions of the ultimate as the One is the conviction of the strong apophatic nature of the ultimate. The resulting apophatic pluralism can appear in different forms: either by resorting to an ultimate silence of which the plurality of religions are true only if they abstain from making dogmatic statements, but instead understand their articulations as mere metaphors of the inexpressible; or by employing paradoxical language to upset any positive one-sidedness of articulation so as to lead to this silence as the true experience in all religions; or by letting the silent ultimate itself go as in deconstructive approaches such as when Jacques Derrida's *différance* remains instead of any ultimate. In fact, this position could be summarized as indicating that there is no ultimate reality, after all, but only the multiplicity of finite beings. It is not so clear to me (even after all the discussions about his work) whether John Hick's pluralistic model is maybe closer to this kind of pluralism, instead (as seems to be the majority opinion, and Hick's text may support this), rather of the third one: the *mystical* solution.

This third solution employs the apophatic nature of God or of the ultimate in a different way, namely, as ultimate Oneness. For this *mystical* pluralism, any positive statement is transformed into symbolisms the ultimate reality of *all* religions, that is, into that which they have in common, but for the price that no religion actually possesses any imagery closer to it than any other. Of course, the more sophisticated understanding of this ultimate One as the true and maybe only Reality will indicate it to reside equally beyond oneness and plurality—that both designations are equally wrong. All religions are inadequate reactions to the One beyond Being, equally right and wrong, but at least this ultimate is truly Reality—even if silent, so nevertheless, being the origin of the different reactions to itself. While one might think that Plotinus' emanationism may be of this sort of thinking, I am not so sure; and I will refer to him presently again suggesting a fourth solution, that of a *polyphilic* pluralism.

In the meantime, let me review the process responses to the pluralistic questions in this general context. I find basically four process responses. First, given the understanding of God's primordial nature as a multiplicity of possible worlds and a diversifying plurality of possibilities for each event in any world (although under the primordial valuation of God's goodness), and given the prehension of the multiplicity of worlds and their diversifications into God's consequent nature, Whitehead speaks of God as a multiplicity (as well as a unity). Hence, we can—for instance with Marjorie Suchocki—claim that God's multiplicity respects, instigates, and wants the world(s) to be diversified, their experiences to be valued in their divergences, and to appreciate different religions—as Whitehead did—as expressions of divine presence. Second, since Whitehead differentiates between several ultimates, several process theologians have variously related the core of different religions to their emphases of one or some ultimates over others. So can John Cobb—in his dialogues with Buddhism—name creativity to indicate the transpersonal ultimate of the *dharmakaya,* and God the ethical dimension of personality highlighted by Christianity. Taking up Cobb's suggestion, David Griffin (and many in the wake of his conceptualization) speaks of the "deep religious pluralism" of process theology—using some version of the set of ultimates used by Whitehead (Exploration 7)—in differentiation from John Hick's apophatic, monistic (identist) pluralism, which only knows of one, although unknowable, ultimate. So Jay Daniels not only elevates the world to the position of an ultimate, but adds one more ultimate, namely, the present moment, so that four kinds of religions could be thought to arise from this view: some religions concentrated on the All and the Earth (indigenous religions), some concentrating on God (theistic religions), some on the interrelatedness of creativity (the abyss of Dharmic religions), and some on the liberating ecstasy of the present moment (as, for instance, in Zen enlightenment experiences). Of course, given the other possible ultimates in Whitehead's thought—such as the realm of potentials and values or the medium of *khora*—there is no end in the potentially infinite proliferation of such ultimates and their theoretical relation to the diversification religious expressions. Third, since several of these ultimates can also be collapsed into one another, the more pantheistic view of Bernard Loomer would prefer not to understand Whitehead's God as an entity different from the world, but would speak of all religions as expression of the web of life of the cosmos as the (divine) mystery that appears differently in different religions. Finally, the naturalistic solution, as favored, for instance, by Bob Mesle, would view Whitehead's God only as a symbol, but understand the ultimacy of the world it indicates to be inherent in it in such a way that always new and different perspectives would be initiated by the creative process, not preferring any religion in the search for the (contextually) "best" symbolism of this mystery.

As for Whitehead, we have already collected and at several points rehearsed the elements that would necessitate religious pluralism in his thought: think, for instance, of the aesthetic character of all experiences as it inherently provides for a diversity of valuation of ultimates and of the categorical grasping of the infinite multiplicity of events and societies; or think of the symbolic character of all experience (at least on a human level) as we experiences beauty, adventure, and peace to indicate ultimacy of meaning and divine theophany; or think of the multiplicity of religions that Whitehead links to the creative imaginations of being liberated from sheer necessity of life and to the ever-new recombinations of solitariness and world solidarity. In relation to polyphilic pluralism, however, I want to point to three further connections between the mystical and the theophanic side of ultimacy and divinity in Whitehead as they relate to theopoetics.

First, it has already been mentioned that, in *Science and the Modern World*, Whitehead understands God as "principle of limitation" insofar as God is not sheer creativity and not sheer potentiality, but the limitation of both by which there can be a value process, a determination necessary for any actual world to arise as fact of values (Exploration 12). In the same context, Whitehead speaks of a "principle of empiricism" by which the actual concretizations, or the actualizations in concrete experiences, of this limitation must appear in the multiplicity of the actual experiences themselves. In other words, by way of divine self-limitation (not to be identical with the infinite ultimates, but to be the actual limitation of their appearance, which therefore must be experientially in the plural) the ultimate must be experienced *variously*—and Whitehead names Yahweh, Allah,

Brahma, Father in Heaven, Order of Heaven, First Cause, Supreme Being, and even Chance as examples. Religious pluralism is a consequence of divine goodness—*the* limitation of God for the process and, at the same time, the limitation of any of its theophanies as unique, but not exhausting expressions of this goodness. Hence, religious pluralism is theopoetic insofar as it is a matter of the aesthetic nature of experience—of the infinite variety of value prehension and value creation in the creative process that is the interaction between infinity and finiteness.

Second, Whitehead's mystical side was introduced mainly through the non-dualistic non-difference between God and the world in the six antitheses of *Process and Reality* (Exploration 8) culminating in the mutual creativeness of God and the world. But it was also already hinted at by the mutual immanence of all ultimates, especially as devised in Whitehead's last lecture "Immortality": the abstraction of the worlds of creativity and value from one another as abstraction from the one universe (Exploration 10). The important point to make, here, is that not only are these worlds related in a non-dual way by mutual immanence (one can only speak of one in symbolic terms by using elements of the other), but that the metaphorical nature of any expression of these worlds are only really understood if they indicate their *specific* non-duality, namely: as that between difference (of creations and values) and non-difference (within their respective ultimates creativity and God). This dialectic is an ancient one. To mention only two instantiations: Plotinus envisioned the One (ultimate reality) as non-differentiated in itself (being neither unity nor multiplicity, but being both and, at the same time, beyond both), but also non-different from its emanations (Divine Mind, World-Soul, and Matter) that indicate the creation process. The apophatic One *is*, at the same time, the All-One. The apophatic Beyond (transcendent to any world and thing) *is*, at the same time, the theophany in all things (immanent to any world and all things)—being none of them, being all of them. Meister Eckhart and Nicolas of Cusa developed this concept further: that the apophatic divinity is different from (and, hence, transcends) the world *precisely* in being non-different (and hence, immanent in) the world. In my book *Prozesstheologie*, I have called that the "absolute transcendence" of God as transcends any dualistic differentiation between God's transcendence and immanence. In *God as Poet of the World*, I have called it the "in-sistence" of God (not "existing" as something within or beyond anything). This final step of this dialectic is left open in Whitehead, but hidden in the mentioned mystical moves of his thought. Yet, if we could, as in Meister Eckhart and Cusanus, speak of God's reality—of absolute transcendence and in-sistence (in)—in Whitehead as being beyond and integrative of both difference *and* non-difference (from creatures), this would be what I have called the *in/difference* of Reality/Truth/God. It indicates more than just a more apophatic term arresting a static ultimate/divine reality. Since it instigates process, it is itself rather a movement, maybe an infinite movement—to use the metaphor of Gilles Deleuze—of which stillness is just an impression hiding infinite activity. In/difference is always in/differentiation, the pulsation (if we slow it down in our symbolic mind) between differentiation and non-differentiation. In/difference is the infinite movement of apophatic self-creativity (in non-difference from anything) and theophanic self-transcendence (into everything). In/difference indicates Realty/Truth/God to be neither mere difference nor mere non-difference, but a third: the apophatic in/differentiation of all that can indicate any difference at all (even that of non-difference) *and*, at the same time and as the same move, the *in-sistence in*, the insisting on *difference*. In/difference is indifferent *from* anything by insisting only *in difference*. Religious pluralism here becomes *polyphilic* as the in/different Reality/Truth/God loves multiplicity. And it indicates divine *insistence* as not being a reality either within or beyond the creative process, but *its* pulsation as multiplicity (although not identical with it at any instance or event). Religions are the subtractive (apophatic) affirmation (theophanies) of Reality/Truth/God beyond, but only within, the multiplicity of religious experiences and their organization (harmonization to heighten their intensity) as permanent recreation of their sensitivity for (the ultimate reality appearing in the midst of the process as) peace.

Third, this polyphilic insistence of divine in/difference, in a last step, indicates a polyphilic pluralism differing from the pragmatic, apophatic, and mystical mysticism with which this exploration has begun. While the pragmatic pluralism is only pluralism by name as it defers its dissolution to God in an eschatological revealing of the true conditions (which are not considered to be pluralistic at all), and while the mystical and the apophatic pluralism waver between an identification of ultimate reality with either the multiplicity of the process or the One beyond, polyphilic pluralism indicates the limit of all of these conceptual movements. Insistence of God means in/difference from, and being only real within, the differences of (religious) experiences and religions. It means to insist on, to *love*, this multiplicity. Hence, divine polyphilia must also *want* the multiplicity of both the theophanic appearances of divinity in different revelations, insights, experiences of salvation and liberation, whether they are personal or transpersonal, *and* the poetic reactions, issuing in diverse religious symbolisms, to its prehension. The in-sistence of God in subtractive affirmation of the multiplicity of religions not only loves to appear differently, but also *values* the theopoetic intuitions arising in these theophanies. Divine theopoetics begets spiritual theopoetics—the theopoetic cycle of love.

Exploration 16

DIVINE MANIFESTATIONS

THE CONCURRENT MOVE OF the apophatic inhalation (in/
difference) and the theophanic exhalation (polyphilia) of
the divine Spirit leads quite naturally to the assumption that
its reality is always only acknowledgeable if it is revealed
in experiences. This means, on the one hand, that we can
know nothing about its "internal" mystery (if we can even
assume such a categorical differentiation between internal
and external to apply to the reality of in/difference) and,
on the other hand, that the different experiences of the
divine it inspires will only appear in divergent religious
experiences, some of them becoming events gathering
religious communities around themselves. Whitehead con-
firms both assumptions. On the one hand, the "principle
of empiricism" of *Science and the Modern World* conveys
the multiplicity of experiences and their creative interpretations as reactions to the theophanic presence (Exploration
15). On the other hand, Whitehead explicates the principle

of mutual immanence when in *Process and Reality* he insists that nothing that leaves the sphere of relationality, that nothing that is beyond connectivity, can be known, and that the unknown is unknowable (Sphere IV). This was the reason that Whitehead in *Adventures of Ideas* militated against the remainder of the Platonic God (with the realm of Ideas) who was considered to be wholly transcendent to the world process, only producing secondary images within the world. It is this immanent transcendence of God that justifies the cycle of love with the categorical differentiations of the natures in God. And it justifies also the theophanic multiplicity with which they are recognized in different religions as expressions of this cycle of love.

This twofold dynamics suggests two consequences. On the one hand, Whitehead can accept the founders of great religious traditions to be theophanies of this polyphilia. At various places, Whitehead names (directly or indirectly), for instance, Moses, Jesus, the Buddha, Mohammad, and Confucius, but also mythological figures such as Prometheus (Exploration 6). They indicate symbolic transfers of experiential structures onto exceptional events (or the converse: of such events onto resonances within patterns of religious experiences) and their recognition within religious societies. These theophanic figures manifest ultimate reality as it is revealed through them in the manifestation of their exceptional experiences, and as they are prehended by these communities gathering around the patterns explicated from them. On the other hand, Whitehead does not assume any ultimate reality beyond the relationality of the process. This again either implies that there is no such reality beyond its immanent transcendence, or that if there is that it is absolutely unknowable. Theopoetic in/difference, however, allows for both views at the same time. This leads us to assume a new apophatic-theophanic structure—that the One is the All-One (Exploration 15)—from a theo-poetic perspective, namely, not only that divine poetics always instigates theopoetic images and symbolisms of its unknown reality, but also that, as it is unreachable, its traces can only be found in the way theophanic figures express its hiddenness in their experiences (and our experiences of them) and, at the same time, upset any hardening of their symbolizations to an reiterated literalism of dogmatic for-mality by an apophatic sublation, a poetic self-subtraction, of the divine, as it appears in differences, into the in/dif-ference beyond any differentiation—both at the same time.

Understood in this way, there are two directions for conceptualizing the theophanic-apophatic double move-ment, namely, either by considering the divine event as the mutual immanence of ultimate reality with the world of process in a "temporal" symbolization, or as a more "spa-tial" symbolism of layers of apophatic subtraction. The first way is indicated by the "temporal process" of the cycle of love, the second by the "spatial presence" of the kingdom of heaven in mutual immanence with the world process or of the divine natures as concurrent layers of reality. Both of these metaphorical symbolizations instantiate a distinctive type of understanding the theophanic-apophatic structure of God's manifestations in the world process, especially in the religiously exceptional figures mentioned before. I will begin by exemplifying the "temporal" way with John Cobb's exploration of Whitehead's process of God's "incarnation" when applied to Christ; then I will add some thoughts on the "spatial" way with a twist on the layered structure of divine "manifestation"—inspired by one of the newest re-ligions exhibiting not only a central concern for religious pluralism, but also an unexpected closeness to Whitehead: the Baha'i Faith.

Whitehead acknowledges, first, divine incarnation as universal phenomenon insofar as the primordial nature is the *eros* at/as the beginning of every new event and, second, that Christ is in Christianity considered the revelation of the nature of God as persuasive movement of love, non-violence, and peace over against the coercive forces of nature and history. In other words, Christ reveals God as highest theophany of the ultimate reality of mutual immanence *in person*. Similar claims could be made of the Buddha—to be the highest manifestation of ultimate relationality (*pratitya-samutpada*) and peace (*nirvana*), the universe being ultimately (of that) Buddha nature. But Cobb explores this Whiteheadian "incarnation" further with the Christ event as he does not understand the Buddha as an expression of (Whitehead's) God, but rather as an expression of (Whitehead's) creativity (Exploration 15). Answering in Whiteheadian terms how this is possible to think coherently, he finds process conceptualizations especially living up to the challenge.

The main idea comprises three interconnected elements. First, as God incarnates in all events, *the* incarnation in Christ is not an exception, but a high point of the theophanic reality of divine immanence. Although this connotes well with current Spirit Christologies—for which Christ is not a preexistent being taking on a body (and soul), but is exceptionally indwelled by the divine Spirit—Cobb rather follows the Gospel of John and its Logos/Wisdom Christology—which has historically also led to the later dogmatic formulations of the Incarnation.

Second, since Whitehead's primordial nature fulfills the function of Wisdom and the Logos in Whitehead's framework (Exploration 8), what must be understood is the special intensity of its presence in Christ to differentiate its theophanic singularity from universal incarnation of it in everything. Cobb finds the differentiating point in the fact that it would, indeed, make all the difference whether the events that constitute the person of Jesus are, as that of everyone else, directed toward the possibilities of every event in its situation and actual world or, as in the Logos become flesh, are directed toward the primordial nature itself, hence, making it part of these events as such, as a whole, in relation to the whole nature and valuation process of God's goodness. In this latter case, one could say that (at least some events of) the life of Jesus were constituted by the Logos, and hence, Jesus was making the Wisdom incarnate in the world process.

Third, it is interesting and significant that this incarnation does not violate the boundaries of the mystery that were formulated dogmatically as being a unity of two natures, the human and the divine, in one person—as neither is violating the properties of the other, but rather is connecting without mixture or separation. Since the initial aim of events that would present the Wisdom of God as a whole would not be different from any other initial aim of any event of the world process or other persons, the primordial nature does neither mix with, nor is it separated from, the person in which it is actualized, nor is the freedom to respond in fulfillment or defiance of this aim taken away from the person of Christ.

As not only Christ, but also the Buddha is said to fulfill in any event (*dharma*) fully the *dharmakaya* and its Dharma, we could connect the primordial and the consequent natures to the fully Enlightened One, too, as an expression of Wisdom and Compassion, respectively. And since there is nothing beyond it, as in Whitehead there is no Godhead beyond these two natures, we could speak of Whitehead's "Godhead" also in terms of a transpersonal "emptiness" (*sunyata*). The fact that Cobb limits the indwelling of Wisdom to Christ as the singular incarnation is then more caused by the interpretation of Christian tradition rather than based on inner necessity of the dynamics of this analysis. In fact, not only have other Christian theologians—such as John Hick, John Macquarrie, and John Haight—made such moves to multiple incarnations, but Whitehead has himself not set any such limit to the workings of the primordial (or the consequent) nature. On the contrary, it seems quite evident that such multiple incarnations or manifestations or theophanies would fit the scheme of the development of religions in Whitehead's works as such theophanic figures inhabit the polyphilic space in which Reality/Truth/God appears in the world as a poetic reality that embraces the bodily universe through creation and salvation. The world is creative of theopoetic imaginations; God is the poetic salvation (transformation) of these creations.

This brings us to the second way for understanding divine Manifestations in terms of the "spatial" image of layers of subtractive in/differentiations of such (theopoetic) imaginations and the divine poetics of the insistence in and on such imaginations (as the symbolic presentations of the theopoetic presence of God in the world process). Not having the space, here, to introduce to the religion as a whole, I will only mention that choosing the Baha'i Faith as an example is based on mainly three groups of inherent process reasons. First, as Whitehead's understanding of God necessitates that eternity must find expression in an aesthetic process of ever-advancing novelty (which he calls the adventure of the universe), this must be true even for the deepest intuitions in the experience in this process, which, for Whitehead, are of a religious nature. Hence, we cannot only expect there to be ever-new manifestations of the Wisdom of God (the primordial nature) in the way Cobb has explored, but we must also be able to recognize them as such. The founders of the Baha'i Faith—the Bab (Seyed Ali Muhammad Shirazi) and Baha'u'llah (Mirza Husayn Ali Nuri)—claim, and are claimed, to be such manifestations and to have inaugurated such a new, independent, and universal religion based on their exceptional religious experiences. As Christianity emerged out of Judaism or Buddhism against its Hindu background, so did the Babi-Baha'i religions arise from (Shi'ite) Islam, but embody a new and unique religious experience and revelation of the nature of ultimate reality (without being able to be reduced to their heritage). And while many religions claim to be the utmost and unsurpassable expression of divine revelation, or ultimate reality, in the world process—Christ as unique, once-and-for-all incarnation, Muhammad as the Seal of all the Prophets, the Sikh Guru Granth Sahib as the last Guru, Krishna as the Ultimate Divine Person—and some of them expect the end of the world process in eschatological manifestations—the second coming of Christ in Christianity, the coming of figures such as Jesus, the Mahdi, the Qa'im, and/ or the last Imam in Sunni and Shi'a Islam—the Baha'i Faith does neither. Neither does it understand its manifestations to be the last ones, nor does it thereby insist on the end of the world process.

Second, as Whitehead's polyphilic intuition about God necessitates always a multiplicity of religions, so does it also gather them into a connex of mutual immanence with one another and with the natures of God. While some religions can only agree to a rhythm of further such manifestations within their own ultimate context—implying future Avatars in Vaishnavism, future Buddhas in Mahayana, future Jinas in Jainism—so as to claim ultimate truth to be revealed through, and, in ultimate analysis, to be confined by, their own series of manifestations, the Baha'i Faith does neither. Instead, it advances the difficult claim that the series of manifestations are to be found distributed throughout *all* religions, such that all religions are originating in, and are reflections of, Truth/Reality/God. For the Baha'i Faith, as for Whitehead, the becoming of religions, the advance into others, the appearance of new ones, is not a matter of syncretism, but of the polyphilic love of God for the multiplicity of the world process in reflecting the infinities of potentials and creativity in inexhaustible finite productions of value facts. But all of them are mutually immanent with one another and united in the divine cycle of love—being the expressions of the *same* primordial nature, being saved by the *same* consequent nature. In fact, in this light, the Baha'i Faith claims that there is in reality only *one* religion, the religion of Reality/Truth/God as mirrored in the infinite process of becoming realized. If Baha'u'llah reveals himself as the Promised One of all religions, this is due to the stage of human history—its global potentials of initiating, and being forced to understand itself in, the unification of the whole planet—rather than the mixture of all religions.

Third, the Baha'i Faith uniquely shares many of the implications and consequences of Whitehead's process universe. I will just mention a few as they relate to the Five Spheres of this book. The Baha'i Faith assumes a cosmology of mutual immanence and processual connectedness (Sphere I). The Baha'i Faith, like Whitehead, believes in the importance of religion and science for the future of civilization and understands the function of religion as the civilizing medium of the unification of humanity beyond any differences of race, color, ethnicity, sex, class, or other prejudicial separation, but as a unity diversified (Sphere II). Like Whitehead, the Baha'i Faith does not assume a beginning and end of the world; rather, it speaks of the beginning that has no beginning and the end that has no end when it wants to address the eternal time involvement of God. It shares the involvement of God in all events of the cosmos of which human history is only one stream, but not the only one. Since the universe is infinite and a multiverse, infinite worlds of God are assumed (Sphere III). Like Whitehead, the Baha'i Faith does not presuppose the uniformity of religious experience, and does not know of any dogmatic fixations of its theological mapping (Sphere IV). And, finally, the Baha'i Faith is theopoetic in nature. It knows of the infinitely many theopoetic imaginations (the imaginal, *alam al-mithal*) creatures intuit of Reality/Truth/God (*al-haqq*), while God is utterly shrouded in apophatic unknowability, even for divine manifestations (Sphere V).

It is also not possible, and necessary, to explore the fascinating details of the Baha'i concept of manifestation (*mazhar-i ilahi*) in relation to notions such as that of the divine incarnation (*logos sarx egeneto*), manifestation (*phaneroustai*), and indwelling (*logos eskenosen*) in Christianity, or else: the full Avatars (*purnavatara*) or divine Manifestations (*pradurbhava*) in Hinduism, the *guru* in Sikhism, the layers of the Buddha bodies (*trikaya*) of Mahayana and the Manifestations (*tulku*) of a *bodhisattva* in Tibetan Buddhism, the theophanies of the Glory of God (*kabod*) in the Sinai event, the Tabernacle, and the *shekinah* in Judaism, or the theophanies (*tajili ilahi*) in the Prophets and Imams in later speculations of Islam. What can be said, however, is this: neither is the Baha'i concept as expounded by Baha'u'llah identical with any of them (as is to be expected if novelty is part of a new religion and its experiences of the divine and ultimate), nor is it so different that it does not connote (at least) a family resemblance with them. In fact, the name Baha'u'llah is also a title, like Christ or the Buddha, and it means Glory, Splendor, Beauty of God (connecting with the *kabod Yahweh* of the Hebrew Bible and the *doxa theou* of the Septuagint and the New Testament). In the Islamic context, it differs, because it is not a mere "revelation" (*tajili*) or "appearance" (*zuhur*), but also not an "incarnation" (*hulul*), which is refused by the majority of the denominations of Islam and only accepted by extreme groups mostly of Shi'ite origin (and so is the incarnation of Christ respectively either denied or accepted by these groups). Nor is it, in a Christian context, a mere "theophany" (or "Christophany"), because it shares the acceptance of the *incarnation* of the Logos and the *two natures* of Christ with Christian scripture and dogma—since the manifestation is of divine and human natures and stations (*lahut* and *nasut*, respectively). The manifestation is concrete and historical (as event and process) like the Christian incarnation (over against the mythological universality of the Hindu *avatara*, and over against the Islamic symbolic interpretation of theophany), but it is also multilayered like the Buddhist *trikaya* (more than the two natures of Christ), and it shares the multiplicity of such theophanic events with the Avatars and Buddhas over against singularity and/or finality of such events in Christianity and Islam as well as Sikhism.

The most interesting element, however, is how it resonates with the divine-mundane dimensions of the cycle of love and, thereby, instantiates the apophatic-theophanic complexity with the theopoetic approach—although with a twist of shedding a new light on Whitehead's horizontal (temporal) cycle by transforming it into a vertical (spatial) map of in/difference. As the Baha'i notion of manifestation reaches deep into Sufi experiences and conceptualizations (while avoiding its pantheistic tendencies), Baha'u'llah's symbolic representations of the apophatic-theophanic axis expresses itself in a version of the layered cosmological scheme that reaches back into Ibn 'Arabi, the great Andalusia philosopher and Sheikh of Sufism—thereby reformulating the apophatic coincidence of opposites (of ultimate reality) found in Meister Eckhart and Nicolas of Cusa, and rehearsing in new ways the emanation scheme of Plotinus (Exploration 15). In Baha'u'llah's version, this scheme symbolically (not literally) conceptualizes the relation of God to the world in five realms of divine differentiation from the absolutely apophatic, undifferentiated (or trans-differentiated) Godhead: *nasut* (the world of humanity, creation, and physical change), *malakut* (the realm of the everlasting kingdom of God), *jabarut* (in Michel Serres's words: the archangelic space, and the divine transhistoric dimension of divine revelation), *lahut* (the realm of manifest divinity, of the Logos, Wisdom, Spirit, Word, Mind, and Will of God), and *hahut* (the inaccessible realm of the unmanifest Godhead).

This is what the symbolism means in our context: on the vertical axis upward, multiplicity and unity increasingly coincide and are transcended into in/difference; on the axis downward, multiplicity and unity are increasingly differentiated in polyphilic diversifications. In the apophatic direction, unification becomes mystical union and beyond that, the in/different expression of divinity and nothingness. That is, the closer a level is to the apophatic Godhead (*hahut*), the more it becomes the pure expression of divinity, manifest only in the nothingness of the medium in which divinity appears such that is reflects nothing but God in its purity. The perfect coincidence of this apophatic-theophanic dialectic, this mutual immanence of non-difference and difference "in" God, is addressed by the reality of the divine Mind, Will, Word, Wisdom, and Spirit of God, the pure manifestation of God (*lahut*). Furthermore, the closer a level is to the theophanic reality of creation (*nasut, alam al-khalq*), the more it reflects the differentiation into diversified (historically embedded, horizontally unique) events of divine revelations, different divine manifestations, and their manifestation in the physical world (like the *trikaya*, but perhaps differing regarding the status of the reality of the physical world). This is how Baha'u'llah understands the humanity (as well as the physical reality) of all manifestations (like Zoroaster, Moses, Jesus, Mohammad, the Buddha, Krishna, the Bab, and Baha'u'llah) to be different, expressing different revelations in different circumstances, and having different personalities, while on the divine levels they are coinherent with one another as transhistorical realities of universal relevance, and, finally, in coincidence, come to be recognized as the expression of the same divine Wisdom and Spirit, Will and Mind of God. This explains why all religions can be true *in* their differentiation (without taking away from their unique universal relevance) and equal, or better, one, in their divine origin—in divine in/differentiation.

With this pattern, we perhaps come closest to the Baha'i understanding of manifestation. First, it means not only the human reality of an inspired prophet or mystic, but embraces all layers of reality between physicality and divinity. Hence, the manifestation is the in-sistence of the unmanifest Godhead in the manifestations of the event process that not only stretches *between* infinite worlds (a multiverse between *nasut* and *lahut*), but on *any* level and in *any* world appears as differentiated reality of *this* level and world (is all-present throughout all worlds). Second, because of the mutual immanence of all levels and their upward increasing in/differentiation, the higher self of the manifestation is at once of prophetic and mystic nature. Respectively, religions cannot be neatly differentiated into prophetic (historic, eschatological, vectorial) and mystic (ahistoric, world-disengaged, and reclusive) religions often schematized as prevailing between the west and the east.

Third, all levels of in/differentiation and in-sistence are expression of the *manifest* God, but are not identical to the apophatic Godhead (like the differentiation between *saguna* and *nirguna brahman*, the wisdom and compassion of the *dharmakaya*, or the named and unnamed *dao*). Fourth, the manifest God (*lahut*) is the perfect nothingness of itself, the spotless mirror in which the apophatic reality (*hahut*) of God is reflected, and reflected into the differences and even oppositions of revelations and intuitions of different religions. This amounts to the paradox (that some Christians would deem kenotic) that the manifestation "is" *only* God by being *not* God (light from light). Fifth, in fact, the manifestation, in this sense, *is* the whole range of the manifest and unmanifest layers of reality, that is, the manifestation of Reality/Truth/God in its in/difference and in-sistence.

Finally, in the Whiteheadian context this symbolic scheme will yield two perhaps unexpected or startling insights. First, since for Whitehead nothing can be unrelated to, and exist beyond, mutual immanence, the apophatic Godhead can, indeed, not be expressed in Whitehead's scheme at all, or not as other than polyphilic in-sistence in the process. In this sense, Whitehead's God with the two natures of the cycle of love engaged with the world is *not* the apophatic Godhead (*hahut*), but the highest reality of *its* manifestation (*lahut*) symbolizing *the* manifestation (*mazhar-i ilahi*). In this sense, Whitehead's leaves the apophatic space to silence. This correlates well with Whitehead's understanding of the primordial nature as Wisdom and Cobb's interpretation of it as Logos, and variously both natures as Wisdom, as well as the consequent nature as Spirit.

Second, the apophatic-theophanic pattern of Whitehead's divine-mundane realities can be expressed in surprising ways by mapping them onto the vertical scheme.

The interaction between this world of process—the world of physical change, and oppositions (all worlds of the multiverse)—and the consequent nature—the kingdom of heavens, the persons in God, the salvation of the process—reflects that of *nasut* and *malakut*, which are also mutually reflective of one another, but differentiated by opposition and change on the one side (*nasut*) and coinherent everlasting transformation on the other (*malakut*). The primordial nature of abstract possibilities and values corresponds to *jabarut*, the realm of abstract powers and valuations of God for the world (God's commands)—transhistorical, abstract, eternal, world-independent, and not fully actual in both cases. *Lahut,* the origin of manifest divinity, reflects Whitehead's contemplation on the root of his God of two natures in the aboriginal, groundless creative act of the *primordial envisagement* of possibilities, potentials, powers, and values, from which height God connects them to meaningful importance and, thereby, instantiates Godself as highest event of groundless creativity. As this process, in Whitehead, ends with the silence of groundlessness as to why this divine process of concrescence is happening at all, we have touched the thick darkness of the cloud of unknowing between the Manifest (*lahut*) and the Unmanifest (*hahut*). Yet, as in Whitehead, we never dwell in this *u-topia* (non-place) as it is unapproachable, as it is only reflected in the in-sistence of God and the theopoetic presence of God in the process of all worlds.

CONTOURS OF BECOMING

LOOKING BACK ON THE process of introducing some of the patterns of Whitehead's thought and Whiteheadian process theology, I want to close by highlighting, first, how the Three Contours To Come of the opening preamble have been addressed and, second, what Contours of Becoming could be released back into the multiplicity of philosophical, theological, and religious discourses.

In the discourse of society, process theology can leave us with potentialities of reflection on the integrity of science and religion, of the importance for, and of, both of them and of a metaphysical dimension of any society that has the impetus to develop globally beyond the oppositions of partial truths and the feeling of superiority of its diverse constituencies to a unity in diversity. Such a plurisingularity could increasingly (but never finally) magnify the aesthetic powers of receptivity to include the mutual immanence of *all* creatures, and it would inspire us to strive for the realization of a *happy* differentiation without opposition that amount to means of mutual destruction, obstruction, and denigration. The feeling of peace is a gift we can tune into as we become attuned to the non-human environment, the foreign society, the stranger, the arbitrary neighbor, the least, the last, and the excluded. Whitehead's philosophy consists not just of a theoretical analysis, but presents us with a lens for *experiencing* the world differently: to experience not only through conceptual reiterations and prejudices (in presentational immediacy), but through feeling the fellow creatures, feeling their way through their life history, and feeling their feeling as spiritual and ethical responsibility, a mandate, really, to change the world in every event anew toward ever-greater sensibility, receptivity, prehensitivity. Process thought directs us to the experiences of every organism, every person, and every society to actually be itself only what it is in the recognition of the transpersonal community the world arouses us to become. We are not alone in this, but may be allowed to experience our in/difference from others in a mysticism and activism of love, compassion, and mutual reciprocity. We may take this feeling of feelings of others (as our feeling, but their becoming) as a basis for resisting non-violently the violence of clashing forces, and we may rediscover religions through Whitehead's lens as saving us from the meaninglessness of a world view and, really, world feeling of hurling blind forces and the mere hopeless suffering of their clashes. That this feeling is not an illusion is what Whitehead tries to instill in us by his intuition of a divine reality or dimension—not as a supreme being far, far above the netherworld of physicality, change, and perpetual perishing, but as immanent in each of its events, in the last puff of existence, and being immanent to them as their very instigation of becoming the subject of their own experiences. That we, in this becoming, also must become objects of others, is not a loss, since we transmit our decisions and values into facts of other's becoming and can learn to feel the failures of our decisions and valuations to be forgiven, transformed, and healed by the all-present event of God, who is the fellow sufferer of our miseries and joys, but also the mirror of our potential greatness. The poetic sense of beauty in our existence will save us from getting stuck in reiterations of past ways of life and will help us to imagine and realize the not-yet of a different future.

In all the talk of becoming and change, the patterns of becoming are equally important. Whitehead seeks not only to revalue the inextricable importance of the events of becoming (over against substantialist isolations), but also to find the eternal in the temporal. He even dedicates his book *Religion in the Making* to this matter. He pursues this intention until his last article "Mathematics and the Good," referring to the correlation of rhythmic patterns in mathematics and poetry to a world process that creates itself inherently from valuations to become as a meaningful network of vibration, of nested fields of aesthetic orders, that cannot be reduced to meaningless facts, empty activities of particles and waves, and dumb matter substances.

Whitehead knows of two ways to void this integrative, concrescent, aesthetic nature of existence. On the one hand, we may become numb to the process in its multiplicity of prehensive influences. He calls this loss of *aesthesis* "anesthesia," and he considers this inability to perceive and creatively imagine a new, more harmonious, and more intense reality the "bastard substitute" for peace. Both anesthesia and peace become independent of the limitations of forces and their suffering. The former fails by shutting down, by becoming imperceptive of reality; the latter succeeds by becoming all-perceptive of reality beyond personal and limited interests. Think of the ideal of the "omniscience" of God in Whitehead, of the Jinas in Jainism, of the Buddhas in Buddhism, and the Manifestations of the Baha'i Faith, as that of the all-suffering, all-perceiving, all-transforming poetics of the in-sistence of ultimate reality.

The other way to obstruct the aesthetic process happens through becoming wasting itself only as a series of fleeting event without any transition into creative accomplishments and their channeling into creative, liberating, and releasing patterns of beauty, adventure, and peace. The modes of self-transcendence of civilization, Whitehead invokes, are modes of such patterns: Adventures, Zest, and Peace. They are not algorithms, because they are poetic; but they do also not exhaust themselves in poetic arbitrariness, but uphold relations—and mathematics, in Whitehead estimation, is the science of their patterns. They express not only formulas, but also the Good, the relations of values in the process of valuation. We live from such patterns; they are our home. From this home base we can venture out to create new realities of harmony and intensity and can bear their transitoriness, and we can enjoy their poetic rhythms in the froth of becoming and perishing. We may even hope to find them again, transformed, in the nature of God, and in surprising ways held for us to reengage with them as we wander along the unknown thrusts of worlds to come. Whitehead calls this transformation the spiritual ascension of the world, the poetic infusion of (mathematical) relations with meaning, importance, and everlastingness, even if the worlds of becoming, and we in it, exhaust themselves physically to the point of seeming non-existence. What is more, Whitehead finds solace in the fact that, even if this world with its creative patterns will fade into just a ripple of the vast sea of forgetfulness, virtually indistinguishable from nonexistence, it is, besides the creativity and inexhaustible potentials of becoming of ever-new worlds, the Wisdom of God that leads this process with divine visions of Truth, Beauty, and Goodness to ever new aesthetic orders.

Not much must be added to the Third Contour of the preamble. That religion and philosophy need one another, and how they can coinhere to expand on the picture already drawn from Whitehead's work and process theologies, has hopefully become evident. I will add only one thought. As no philosophy can exhaust the metaphysical structures gleaned from, critically accompanying, and releasing us into a multireligious world, of course, even Whitehead's philosophy is just one possibility among many, but not infinitely many, as it is based on experiences that, if they cannot be had or change in unintended or surprising directions, will fade like the worlds that cease to instantiate their cosmic structures. Its justification is our experience. Not all developments following from this fading need to be an advance; some, or many, may, indeed, just be worse. Anesthesia always lingers. It is, however, at our own peril that we waste good alternatives in philosophy and religion, not only open to us as possibility, but confronting us as event, as *kairos*. Even more so, it is irresponsible to not improve on them in directions that are more beautiful, more adventurous, and more peaceful. This also assumes that, as neither philosophy nor religion are static entities, *change* is necessary and good, as it also reflects back on social and cultural relativity and alteration. Advancement in civilization will always be critical—born in crisis and undergoing a catharsis of novelty. Nevertheless, we blind ourselves if we assume that there is only (aimless) process, and no potentials of a (purposive) progress. Not the progress of capitalism, scientism, or one towards a globalism of total security and control, and so on, but the progression into world-sensibility, the expanding feeling of peace, and a venturing into the multiple directions by which religious experiences can lead us closer to a unity in diversity. This is not mere relativism, then, but teleology without final aim, or it is

sensibility toward final aims without negation of their processual impermanent immanence. It is this sensibility by
which Whitehead thinks that any sophisticated organism
survives not just for survival's sake. In the mystical sensitivity to even remote potentials of becoming and the prophetic
sensitivity to a future yet beyond imagination, sur-vival (*sur
vivre,* super-vivere, in Derrida's understanding), becomes
"more than life," becomes part of the divine process, a "living fact" for the multiplicity of becoming alive in the Spirit.

If I can now visualize the whole of this endeavor to access sensibly the potentials inherent in Whitehead's thought
and in process theologies, I would say that they try to integrate these three modes of becoming: the God of becoming, the becoming of God, and the becoming of becoming.
God is a God *of* becoming. God cares for interconnection,
but not for a halt. God cares for process, but not for wasting time with the hollow numbness of frozen sculptures.
How can God care for anything less than process if God
is God and not a mere image of our failed imaginations?
God is *in* becoming. Mind you, God does not change, but
God becomes with the world. God is not as the victim of
the creative process, but as its champion, in the sovereignty
of love that suffers all and transfigures all. How can God's
eternity be less than all-perceptive and all-creative if God
is God and not a figment of our failed imagination? And
the world, the universe, the multiverse of all worlds that
have become, become now, and will become, are instances,
maybe even *themselves* "events" of becoming. Becoming,
in this sense, after all the search for an ultimate ground or
reality of realities, really has no ground. It is its own ground.
In *Adventures of Ideas,* Whitehead calls this groundless
ground "Immanent Self-Creativity." In this groundlessness,
we need not functionalize God or heaven or eternity for our
escape from becoming or to find an inviolable foundation.

Instead, if the becoming of becoming is the ground of becoming, all related events of becoming *are* the ultimate.
The ultimate becomes the *medium*. And in this medium of
becoming, nothing shines through but an ultimate reality,
unspeakable, unknowable, absolutely apophatic, yet itself
in/different from, and in-sisting as love, the polyphilia of
becoming.

RECOMMENDED READINGS

Bracken, Joseph. *The Divine Matrix: Creativity as a Link between East and West*. New York: Orbis, 1995.

Cobb, John B. *A Christian Natural Theology: Based on the Thought of Alfred North Whitehead*. Louisville: Westminster John Knox, 2007.

———. *Christ in a Pluralistic Age*. Eugene, OR: Wipf & Stock, 1999.

Cobb, John B., and David Griffin. *Process Theology: An Introductory Exposition*. Louisville: Westminster John Knox, 1976.

Dean, William, and Larry Axel Macon, eds. *The Theology of Bernard Loomer in Context*. Macon, GA: Mercer University Press, 1987.

Deleuze, Gilles. *The Fold: Leibniz and the Baroque*. Minneapolis: University of Minnesota Press, 1992.

Epperly, Bruce G. *Process Theology: A Guide for the Perplexed*. Guides for the Perplexed. New York: Bloomsbury, 2011.

Faber, Roland. *God as Poet of the World: Exploring Process Theologies*. Louisville: Westminster John Knox, 2008.

———. *The Divine Manifold*. Lanham, MD: Lexington, 2014.

———. *Prozesstheologie. Zu ihrer Würdigung und kritischen Erneuerung*. Mainz: Matthias Grünewald Verlag, 2000.

Faber, Roland, and Jeremy Fackenthal, eds. *Theopoetic Folds: Philosophizing Multifarious-ness*. New York: Fordham University Press, 2012.

Faber, Roland, and Andrea Stephenson, eds. *Secrets of Becoming: Negotiating Whitehead, Deleuze, and Butler*. New York: Fordham University Press, 2010.

Faber, Roland, and Santiago Slabodsky, eds. *Living Traditions and Universal Conviviality: Prospects and Challenges for Peace in Multireligious Communities*. Lanham, MD: Lexington, 2016

Recommended Readings

Ford, Lewis. *Transforming Process Theism*. Albany: State University of New York Press, 2000.

Ford, Lewis, and George Kline, eds. *Explorations in Whitehead's Philosophy*. New York: Fordham University Press, 1983.

Griffin, David R. *God, Power, and Evil: A Process Theodicy*. Philadelphia: Westminster, 1976.

✓ ———. *Reenchantment without Supernaturalism: A Process Philosophy of Religion*. Ithaca, NY: Cornell University Press, 2001.

Griffin, David R., ed. *Deep Religious Pluralism*. Louisville: Westminster John Knox, 2005.

Hartshorne, Charles. *Omnipotence and Other Theological Mistakes.* Albany: State University of New York Press, 1984.

———. *The Divine Relativity: A Social Conception of God*. New Haven, CT: Yale University Press, 1948.

Hosinski, Thomas. *Stubborn Fact and Creative Advance: An Introduction to the Metaphysics of Alfred North Whitehead*. Lanham, MD: Rowman and Littlefield, 1993.

Keller, Catherine. *The Cloud of the Impossible*. New York: Columbia University Press, 2015.

———. *Face of the Deep: A Theology of Becoming*. New York: Routledge, 2003.

———. *On the Mystery: Discerning God in Process*. Minneapolis: Fortress, 2008.

Kraus, Elisabeth. *The Metaphysics of Experience: A Companion to Whitehead's Process and Reality*. New York: Fordham University Press, 1998.

Lucas, George R., Jr. *The Rehabilitation of Whitehead: An Analytic and Historical Assessment of Process Philosophy*. Albany: State University of New York Press, 1989.

McDaniel, Jay. *Gandhi's Hope: Learning from Other Religions as a Path to Peace*. Maryknoll, NY: Orbis, 2005.

McDaniel, Jay, and Donna Bowman, eds. *Handbook of Process Theology*. St. Louis: Chalice, 2006.

Mesle, Robert. *Process Theology: A Basic Introduction*. St. Louis: Chalice, 1993

Odin, Steve. *Process Metaphysics and Hua-Yen Buddhism: A Critical Study of Cumulative Penetration vs. Interpenetration.* Albany: State University of New York Press, 1982.

Ogden, Schubert. *The Reality of God and Other Essays*. Dallas: Southern Methodist University Press, 1992.

Rose, Philip. *On Whitehead.* Belmont, CA: Wadsworth, 2002.

Recommended Readings

Schilpp, Paul, ed. *The Philosophy of Alfred North Whitehead*. La Salle, IL: Open Court, 1991.

Shaviro, Steven. *Without Criteria: Kant, Whitehead, Deleuze, and Aesthetics*. Cambridge, MA: MIT Press, 2009.

Stengers, Isabelle. *Thinking with Whitehead*. Cambridge, MA: Harvard University Press, 2012.

Suchocki, Marjorie. *Divinity and Diversity: A Christian Affirmation of Religious Pluralism*. Nashville: Abington, 2003.

———. *God, Christ, Church: A Practical Guide to Process Theology*. New York: Crossroad, 1995.

Whitehead, Alfred N. *Adventures of Ideas*. New York: Free Press, 1967.

———. *Essays in Science and Philosophy*. New York: Greenwood, 1975.

———. "Immortality." In Alfred N. Whitehead, *Essays in Science and Philosophy*, 77–96. New York: Greenwood, 1975.

———. "Mathematics and the Good." In Alfred N. Whitehead, *Essays in Science and Philosophy*, 97–113. New York: Greenwood, 1975.

———. *Modes of Thought*. New York: Free Press, 1968.

———. *Process and Reality: An Essay in Cosmology*. Edited by D. R. Griffin and D. W. Sherburne. New York: Free Press, 1978.

———. *Religion in the Making*. New York: Fordham University Press, 1996.

———. *Science and the Modern World*. New York: Free Press, 1967.

———. *Symbolism: Its Meaning and Effect*. New York: Fordham University Press, 1985.

———. *The Concept of Nature*. Cambridge: Cambridge University Press, 1993.

———. *The Function of Reason*. Boston: Beacon, 1958.

———. *A Treatise on Universal Algebra: With Applications*. Cambridge: Cambridge University Press, 1898.

Wilmot, Laurence. *Whitehead and God: Prolegomena to a Theological Reconstruction*. Waterloo, ON: Wilfrid Laurier University Press, 1979.

INDEX OF CONCEPTS

INDEX OF PERSONS

Index of Persons

Made in the USA
Middletown, DE
19 December 2021

56592172R00154